Acquiring Competency and Achieving Proficiency with

DIALECTICAL BEHAVIOR THERAPY

Volume II
The Worksheets

Cathy Moonshine, Ph.D., MAC, CADC III

PESI®

EAU CLAIRE, WISCONSIN

Implementing Dr. Moonshine's DBT in Life™ worksheets has enabled me to provide my clients with skills that provide a construct to build a life worth living. The materials are oriented toward learning and developing a skill set that are relevant to life experiences and provide examples that are concrete and relative. I have found this approach to Dialectical Behavior Therapy to be valuable and helpful to clinicians to help facilitate client skill building for a better life.

Tracy McDowell, M.A.
Private Practice

Dr. Moonshine's new book balances the dialectic between theory and practice. This book answers the call for a reproducible curriculum that can ease the burden of the therapist and the client. Dr. Moonshine makes a complicated theory immediately available for application, getting the necessary activities and exercises into the hands of therapists and into the lives of those suffering unbalanced mental health.

Jesse Crotty, M.A.
Clinician @ Green Door

We have been using the DBT in Life worksheets with our young clients and it's been extremely useful. It seems that my colleagues and myself have been looking for a modified curriculum in "teenspeak" especially one that addresses DBT in a more lively, active format—not just cognitive. The worksheets, activities and games been really invaluable.

Jen Leland, LMFT
Clinician @Walden House

As a counselor working with problem gamblers here, I've found Cathy's workbook to be useful with a number of my clients. The DBT skills are clearly explained, and the worksheets make them applicable in both group and individual sessions.

Travis Kerns, MA, CADC I, CGAC II
Clinician @ Cascadia Behavioral Healthy & in Private Practice

After using Dr. Moonshine's resources I am thinking about how to make DBT interventions with an African American focus in my private practice. Thanks, for the inspiration!

Kathy Williams, LCSW
Director of Social Services @ Montevista Hospital

The worksheets contained in Vol. II have been created in such a way that both clinicians new to DBT and those who have been practicing DBT for years can use these worksheets to effectively teach DBT to clients. The information in Vol. I is complimented by the excellent, user-friendly worksheets in Vol. II, creating a well-rounded set of materials for all who want to learn and practice DBT. The format of separating the instructional materials and the client materials makes this pair of books invaluable to clinicians and allows clients the opportunity to purchase their own "workbooks" instead of depending on the clinician to have the resources and time to make their own worksheets or workbooks.

Stephanie Schaefer, MA, Psy.D. Student
School of Professional Psychology @ Pacific University.

"Where ever you go, there you are."

I would like to acknowledge important people in my life that taught me about being skillful, even if we didn't know it at the time.

My mother, Claire, taught me about "Turtling" by using variety of strategies to take care of herself such as being adaptive, resilient and persistently self righting.

Nikki & Bruce taught me about "Effectively", "Crisis Survival Network," and "Turning the Mind" which changed my life course.

Matt demonstrates the usefulness of irreverent communication nearly every day. He also employs the skills of "Ride the Wave", "CARES" and "Broken Record" regularly.

Martin & Andre demonstrate the importance of "Keeping It In Perspective" and "SPECIFIC PATHS."

Looking towards what the future holds for my nephew William and niece Margo. Here's to making "Lemonade", being in "Wise Mind" and a little bit of "Radical Acceptance."

A special expression of gratitude is given to all that contributed to my proficiency with DBT. In particular, thanks are offered to Tracy, Emily, Erica & Emily.

Thanks to Mike and Linda for giving me countless opportunities over the years to expand my DBT expertise along with encouragement to write these books.

For all who assisted me in the creation and refinement of the DBT texts: S.S., R.S., J.C., T.M., V.H., T.H., C.S., D.C., M.R., C.P., T.K., Y.S., & M.C.

PESI, LLC
PO Box 1000
3839 White Avenue
Eau Claire, Wisconsin 54702

Printed in the United States of America

ISBN: 978-0-9790218-5-5

PESI, LLC strives to obtain knowledgeable authors and faculty for its publications and seminars. The clinical recommendations contained herein are the result of extensive author research and review. Obviously, any recommendations for patient care must be held up against individual circumstances at hand. To the best of our knowledge any recommendations included by the author or faculty reflect currently accepted practice. However, these recommendations cannot be considered universal and complete. The authors and publisher repudiate any responsibility for unfavorable effects that result from information, recommendations, undetected omissions or errors. Professionals using this publication should research other original sources of authority as well.

For information on this and other PESI manuals and
audio recordings, please call 800-843-7763 or
visit our website at www.pesi.com

Table of Contents

About the Author

Cathy Moonshine, PhD, MAC, CADC III is the Executive Director of a private consulting firm, Moonshine Consulting as well as assistant professor at the School of Professional Psychology at Pacific University in Portland, Oregon. Dr. Moonshine is an expert trainer, clinical supervisor and clinician. In 2007, Dr. Moonshine created and published DBT board game, playing cards, bingo, and bonanza dice game. All of these and other resources are available at the D.B.T. in Life™ Store at http://www.Moonshine-Consulting.com.

Dr. Moonshine is largely self-taught in Dialectic Behavior Therapy ("DBT"). She has read many books and professional articles on DBT and has utilized clinical supervision and consultation with colleagues to increase her competency with this model. Dr. Moonshine completed her doctoral education at Pacific Graduate School of Psychology in Palo Alto, CA. She received her Master's from Seattle University and Bachelor's from University of Redlands.

Dr. Moonshine has modified DBT to work with clients, graduate students, supervisees, and in program oversight. Dr. Moonshine focuses on balancing dialectics, being mindfully present, and making use of DBT skills. The DBT skills that Dr. Moonshine utilizes in her work include ones originally created by Dr. Marsha Linehan and/or other authors. Dr. Moonshine has sought to utilize the most successful aspects of the traditional DBT model in combination with her own successful treatment philosophies, patient methods, and teaching skills.

Dr. Moonshine acknowledges with gratitude Dr. Linehan as the creator of the DBT model. However, all trainings, clinical support, and products created or sold by Dr. Moonshine are of her own creation without collaboration with Dr. Linehan, or Dr. Linehan's affiliated company, Behavioral Tech, LLC. Dr. Moonshine's products are not sanctioned by, sponsored, licensed, or affiliated with Dr. Linehan and/or Behavioral Tech, LLC. Clinicians and programs interested in providing full fidelity to the empirically supported DBT protocol and wishing to be recognized as official DBT clinicians should contact Behavioral Tech at http://www.behavioraltech.org or (206) 675-8588.

Dr. Moonshine has over twenty years of experience in public and private mental health and substance abuse treatment settings across all levels of care. Dr. Moonshine provides licensure supervision and collegial consultation to mental health, addictions and dual diagnosis clinicians. She works with systems of care and individual clinicians to implement and sustain evidenced based practices. Dr. Moonshine serves as Clinical

Director for nearly 10 years in Portland, Oregon. In addition to Clinical Director duties, Dr. Moonshine continues to make an impact in the local, state and national treatment communities with her consultation, supervision and trainings. Dr. Moonshine is considered an expert in the areas of addictions and dual diagnosis treatment.

CHAPTER 1
Overview of DBT

DBT BACKGROUND

DBT stands for Dialectical Behavior Therapy, which was created by Marsha Linehan, Ph.D. This therapy model has been significantly researched and validated to be effective with a variety of serious mental health concerns. Dr. Linehan has created many useful resources facilitating competence with DBT including: *Cognitive-Behavioral Treatment Of Borderline Personality Disorder, Skills Training Manual For Treating Borderline Personality Disorder,* and *The Freedom from Chaos* video series. Recent publications by Dr. Linehan's colleagues are *Dialectical Behavior Therapy With Suicidal Adolescents* by Alec Miller et al, as well as *Dialectical Behavior Therapy In Clinical Practice: Applications Across Disorders And Settings* edited by Linda Dimeff and Kelly Koerner. Visit http://www.behavioraltech.org for more information about these and other resources.

The "D" in DBT stands for Dialectical. Dialectics are things that seem to be in conflict and yet they are both real or true. The term comes from philosophy, and is used to illustrate that there is usually a kernel of truth in each perspective in a dialogue or argument, even when there is a difference of opinion or belief. Being dialectical is seeing that reality is black, white and a lot of shades of gray. It's when there is one more than one right answer, sometimes there is no good answer and every now and then individuals have to pick the lesser of two evils. Dialectics can be balancing self and others, giving and getting, needs and wants, work and play, winning and losing, etc.

Dialectics can be seen on TV and heard in popular music almost every day. Many popular song lyrics illustrate dialectics. A few examples of lyrics from both songs that are illustrations of dialectics are below:

Examples from "Ironic" by Alanis Morissette:

> *It's winning the lottery & dying the next day*
> *It's a death row pardon two minutes too late*
> *It's like rain on your wedding day*
> *It's the good advice that you just didn't take*
> *It's a traffic jam when you're already late*
> *It's a no-smoking sign on your cigarette break*

Take a look at "Waterfalls" by TLC:

A lonely mother gazing out of her window,
Staring at her son that she just can't touch
If at any time he's in a jam,
She'll be by his side,
But he doesn't realize he hurts her so much
I seen a rainbow yesterday,
But too many storms have come and gone

A third musical example is "Love Me if You Can" by Toby Keith:

Sometimes I think that war is necessary
Every night I pray for peace on Earth
I hand out my dollars to the homeless
But believe that every able soul should work
I stand by my right to speak freely
But I worry 'bout what kids learn from TV
Before all of debating turns to angry words & hate
Sometimes we should just agree to disagree
Call me wrong, call me right
Hate me if you want to
Love me if you can

Check out "Leave Me Alone" By Pink:

Go away,
Give me a chance to miss you
I love you so much more when you're not here
I'm tired, leave me alone
I'm lonely,
Alone I'm lonely tonight
Go away, come back,
Go away, come back,
Why can't I just have it both ways
Go away, come back,
Go away, come back,
I wish you knew the difference

Another musical example is "Just Like a Boy" by CIARA:

Tell you I love you,
But when you call I never get back
Can't be get'n mad! What You Mad? Can't Handle that!
Keep a straight face when ya tell a lie,
Always keep an airtight alibi
Keep him in the dark,
What he don't know won't break his heart

Nelly Furtado has dialectics in her "Say It Right" song:

You either got it or you don't,
You either stand or you fall
Oh you don't mean nothing at all to me,
No you don't mean nothing at all to me
But you got what it takes to set me free,
Oh you could mean everything to me
I can't say that I'm not lost and at fault,
I can't say that I don't love the light and the dark

Another musical example is "Take Me As I Am" by Mary J. Blige:

She's been down and out,
She's been up and down
She has no regrets,
She accepts the past.
All these things they helped make to make she
She's been lost and found
And she's still around
Try to make me weak,
But I still stay strong,
She's on solid ground

Nickelback's "If Everyone Cared" song that illustrates a few dialectics:

If everyone cared and nobody cried
If everyone loved and nobody lied
If everyone shared and swallowed their pride
And as we lie beneath the stars.
We realize how small we are

"With or Without You" by U2 also contains examples of dialectics:

> *Through the storm we reach the shore*
> *You give it all but I want more,*
> *And I'm waiting for you*
> *I can't live with or without you*
> *Nothing to win and*
> *Nothing left to lose*

A final musical example is "Nothing About Love Makes Sense" by Leann Rimes song:

> *Like a cloud full of rain shouldn't hang in the sky*
> *Ice shouldn't burn or a bumblebee fly*
> *Like an ocean liner shouldn't float on the sea*
> *That big Italian tower, well how does it lean?*
> *Like the lights of Las Vegas going out on the sand*
> *A jumbo shrimp or a baby grand*

Other examples of dialectics that happen in the real world:

- Wanting financial stability while having debt
- Wanting fewer problems while sometimes making life worse than it needs to be
- Wanting to be thin but overeating
- Wanting to avoid trouble while breaking rules or committing crimes
- Wanting to be treated like an adult while acting like a child
- Wanting to be loved and cared about while pushing people away
- Wanting independence while being dependent on others
- Wanting a simple life during a time of enormous technology

Ineffective dialectics may be:

- Wanting to be loved and staying in a violent relationship
- Having compassion for others while hating oneself
- Asking for help and not accepting the help
- Having a lot of anxiety and ingesting enormous amounts of caffeine and/or nicotine
- Trying to manage depression through the use of alcohol and/or other drugs
- Wanting to prevent mental health symptoms but not taking medication as directed

With any ineffective dialectics, individuals will benefit from using DBT to achieve balance with their competing needs. By using their DBT skills, they can move away from extremes of their current dialectics. DBT consists of four content areas: *Mindfulness, Distress Tolerance, Emotional Regulation*, and *Interpersonal Effectiveness.*

> *Mindfulness* is about being in the here and now most of the time. It's about doing one thing at a time. When individuals use mindfulness in their lives, they are able to stay in balance, remain nonjudgmental and be as effective as possible.

> *Distress Tolerance* is about learning to tolerate frustration. It's about being able deal with stress, drama, and crises in skillful ways.

> *Emotional Regulation* is about learning impulse control. This includes tolerating, managing and coping with emotions, impulses, urges and cravings while not acting automatically or without thinking it through.

> *Interpersonal Effectiveness* is about being effective in relationships. Here individuals balance investment in relationships, commitment to self and the ability to communicate effectively.

DEVELOPING BALANCED TRAVELS IN LIFE™

DBT in Life™ products have been created by Cathy Moonshine, Ph.D., MAC, CADC III and distributed through Moonshine Consulting.com. DBT in Life products are based on Dialectical Behavior Therapy. These products include games, posters, annual calendar, and incentives. DBT in Life products™ are designed to educate people about how DBT skills can enhance their ability to effectively deal with stress and troubles. On the one hand, these skills can be very useful for individuals with significant problems and difficulties. On the other hand, these skills are useful in optimizing functioning and life satisfaction for individuals who are relatively well adjusted and self actualized.

Developing Balanced Travels in Life™ is about being able to tolerate and effectively manage life's inherent confusions, paradoxes and ironies. It is about avoiding extremes, such as "people are either with me or against me," "all or nothing," "lots of work and no play," "it's all about me and who cares what others want," or unhealthy lifestyles that lack any elements of self-care. Being balanced in life is about a "both/and" perspective instead of an "either/or" perspective. Individuals may have friends and families that support them while disagreeing with them sometimes. People can work hard and enjoy life. Folks can take of themselves and help others. Individuals can engage in problematic behavior while maintaining healthy self-care. People will probably experience more life satisfaction, sustain healthier relationships and achieve more of their goals when they are able to balance the dialectics of their lives. Many of the suggestions in this section will apply to teaching DBT skills, other skills, or other psychoeducational models. Learning needs to be accessible, relevant, engaging, fun, and interesting. Two major considerations of teaching skills are learning styles and attention span.

LEARNING STYLES:

Children, teenagers, and adults learn three ways: auditorally, visually, and kinesthetically, and each person has a preferred style or way that he learns best. Some clients learn best by listening and talking about things. These clients are primarily auditory learners. Other clients will learn best through reading and visual representations. These clients are primarily visual learners. The last group includes clients whose optimal learning state happens through doing things, being active, and practicing things in their lives. These clients are kinesthetic learners. While each person has a preferred style or way they learn best, most clients can benefit from learning new concepts through a variety of styles.

When teaching DBT skills it is important to appeal to all three of these styles. Lecture or discussion about the skills is helpful and using visual representations of skills through media, posters, or objects is recommended.

Auditory learning activities	Visual learning activities	Kinesthetic learning activities
Lecture	Written handouts	Art projects
Discussion	PowerPoint presentation	Games
Small-group exercises	Art projects	Role plays
	Games	Small group exercises

Perhaps the most important component of learning DBT is practice. Clients should practice the skills in the session, whether it is individual or group, as well as in their lives outside the therapy room or treatment program. There is a difference between knowing a skill and using a skill. Some clients can learn skills quickly and may be able to provide a more sophisticated explanation of the skill than the clinician. They may even coach or give advice to their peers. All of this can happen without the client practicing the skill in his life on a consistent basis.

ATTENTION SPAN:

While in some ways teenagers may have the capacity to pay attention longer than adults, both teenagers and adults have limited attention spans. Some clients have very long attention spans. Some activities can engage the attention span for an extended amount of time while other activities are only able to engage the attention span for a few minutes or seconds. When teaching the skills it is optimal to have a variety of activities. Don't do any one activity for too long. If the clinician is bored with an activity the clients may be bored as well. Activities to try:

- A little bit of lecture
- Video and music examples
- Handouts
- Small group activities
- Skits and charades
- Art work such as painting, model, or making collages

- Having the clients teach one another a skill
- Imagery and visualizations
- Role plays and in vivo practice
- Guest speaker

Observe and learn from the clients, and use what works for them. learn from professional colleagues as well. Inquire how other clinicians teach skills, watch other clinicians work, or invite other clinicians to the group. DBT is hard work and having fun is a useful way to make it engaging and interesting. Additional components to consider when teaching DBT skills include fostering motivation, tools that foster learning, and Cognitive-Behavioral interventions. Practice and homework assignments outside the individual or group therapy session are essential if clients are going to be successful in utilizing their DBT skills in real life situations.

CLIENT WORKSHEETS

Chapters 3–7 contain more than 150 worksheets to assist you in teaching DBT skills to clients. This is probably more than any one clinician can use effectively and considerably more than any one client will need. There is at least one worksheet for every skill. In some cases there are multiple worksheets. The clinician is encouraged to review the worksheets and pick the ones that resonate with him or her based on clinical style, client need, and setting. The multiple worksheets provide a variety of skills and teaching methods. Hopefully, this keeps the practice of teaching skills fresh, interesting, and creative. The worksheets can be used in a variety of contexts including individual sessions, group therapy, therapeutic communities, classrooms, or as homework assignments.

These worksheets are designed to provide structure and ideas about how to teach the skills to clients. The worksheets provide basic information about the skills to clients. Most of the handouts provide an opportunity for clients to write out how they could use a skill, barriers, and obstacles to using the skill and strategies to overcome the barriers. By exploring the skills in writing, clients are better able to retain what the skills mean and how they can use them in their lives.

The worksheets are designed to appeal to all three learning styles: visual, auditory, and kinesthetic. As you are using the worksheets, remember to make learning fun and interesting. Through use of the worksheets, clients will learn how the skills are relevant for them. Through the client's self-interest and the realization that the skills will be useful for them, it will build motivation for them to use the skills on a regular basis in their lives.

Some of the skills have more than one worksheet. In most cases, multiple worksheets for the same skill are provided because a skill is complex or so important that it requires more than one worksheet. The other reason for multiple worksheets is to give the clinician a variety of options to choose from for teaching the skill to the client.

When using the worksheets in individual sessions you can read the handout silently or out loud. Then facilitate a discussion of the skill. If there are prompts, have the client fill out the handout. If the client can't or won't fill out the handout, fill in their answers for them. You can ask clients how they can use the skill in their lives. If they can't think of any ways to use it, perhaps you could offer some suggestions. Take a couple of minutes to explore how using the skill might be difficult or challenging along with ways to reduce or eliminate these challenges. Finally, you can give the clients the assignment to use the skill as often as possible before the next time you see them.

In group sessions you can facilitate a similar process of discussing and completing the worksheet either with the large group as a whole or by breaking them into small groups. After completing the handout in small groups, each group can share all or part of what they talked about and/or wrote down. Then discuss problems, solutions, and the assignment to practice the skill in their lives. These worksheets can be used in classrooms in same fashion as group therapy.

In the therapeutic community, clients can complete these worksheets on their own time. They can compare notes with other clients and any milieu staff.

Giving the worksheets as homework provides opportunities for clients to continue working on their goals and increasing their skills between sessions. Take a few minutes in the session to give the client the worksheet, ask him or her to review it, and then answer any questions he or she may have. Clarify the directions and ask the client to bring the worksheet back the following week. Be prepared to give them another copy if they forget. When assigning homework, it is essential that you check to make sure they completed it and see if they learned anything from it. If the client has not done the homework, you can assign it again. In some cases, clients still won't do the homework. In these cases, have the client do the homework in session. After doing this once or twice most clients will realize that you are serious about the homework and begin completing it between sessions.

Many of the worksheets have space for clients to write responses. If more space is needed, they can write on the back of the worksheet or use an additional sheet of paper. Remind clients that there can be more than one right answer so that they don't feel that they have to do it perfectly.

COMMENTS ON SPECIFIC WORKSHEETS.

There are several "pros and cons" exercises:

- Pros and cons of staying the same or changing
- Pros and cons of participating in DBT
- Pros and cons of using skills
- Pros and cons of completing homework
- Pros and cons of using diary cards
- Pros and cons of therapy-interfering behavior
- Pros and cons of drama and crisis
- Pros and cons of changing relationships

These are not the only possible "pros and cons" exercises; you can create your own. For this you will find a blank "pros and cons" form later in the chapter. Sometimes language doesn't fit for the clinician or the client. For this reason there are blank forms in the same format but instead of "Pros and Cons," it is "Cost Benefit Analysis" or "Positive and Negatives."

You may use all of these pros and cons multiple times. The "length and intensity" of answers in each box will give you an indication of the client's stage of change with regard to the focus of the pros and cons. If the client has a long list or important things on the top row, but little or nothing on the bottom row, the client is likely to be in pre-contemplation or early contemplation. If there is balance in the top and bottom, then the client is likely to be in contemplation. When the lists are longer or more intense in the bottom, the client is probably in preparation and action.

In Chapter 3 there are two calendar templates. Clients may put a sticker or star on each day that they use a skill. You might not think that teenagers and adults will enjoy this activity, but they often do. Try it out with a few clients to see how they react. If you think of another way to use the calendars that reinforces the use of skills, feel free to use that instead.

Diary cards, simple chain analysis, and in-depth chain analysis are included in Chapter 3. You will also find worksheets to prevent relapses and plans for recovery. For detailed instructions and examples of how to use these tools, see *Volume I: Clinician's Guidebook.*

There are a few handouts that leave space for the clients to draw or do artwork. These include the **Turtling** and **Turning the Mind** worksheets. Even though there aren't worksheets to do with other skills, you certainly can. These skills would include **Lemonade, Love Dandelions, Ride the Wave,** and many others. These can be used in art therapy or with creative clients. Clients may also want to color or doodle on other worksheets. This is perfectly acceptable.

At the end of Chapter 3 you will find a DBT crossword puzzle and answer sheet. In the remaining four chapters you will find a crossword puzzle and word search along with answer sheets for each of the four skills categories. These can be used at the end of teaching each category in session or as homework after the client has learned many of the skills.

To see electronic copies of the worksheets in either black and white or full color, visit the DBT in Life™ store at http://www.Moonshine-Consulting.com. You may download them for a nominal fee. There are many other resources available at this website as well. Feel free to copy worksheets printed in this book or downloaded from the website as needed for clinical purposes. You may also use these worksheets as a jumping-off point to create your own. Use the worksheets in any way that will help your clients learn and use DBT skills in their lives. In addition to the worksheets in this book, you can also find worksheets in *DBT Skills Training Manual* by Marsha Linehan and *DBT in Private Practice* by Thomas Marra. You may also find self-help books such as *Don't Let Emotions Run Your Life* by Scott Spradlin, *Depressed and Anxious* by Thomas Marra or *DBT Workbook* by Matthew McKay and others currently in print to be helpful.

Remember, there are more handouts than a single clinician or program can use or that a client would be able to absorb. Review the handouts. Become familiar with them. Use the ones that resonate with you. If clients are in treatment for an extended time, the variety of handouts will be useful in giving them new and different ways to reinforce the meaning of the skills and the importance they have in the clients' lives.

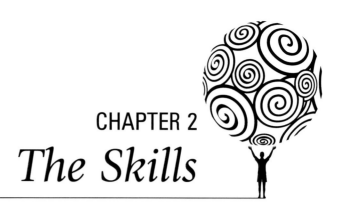

CHAPTER 2
The Skills

DBT consists of four content areas: Mindfulness, Distress Tolerance, Emotional Regulation, and Interpersonal Effectiveness. A fifth module, the Middle Path, is for teenagers and their families. It doesn't have its own set of skills, but pulls skills from the other four modules to instill balance in families (Miller, Rathus.& Linehan, 2006).

There are a number of traditional, or "classic," DBT skills created by Dr. Linehan (Linehan 1993a; Linehan, 1993b). There are also innovative skills created by other authors, including the one producing this text (Marra, 2004; Moonshine, 2007; Spradlin, 2003). These skills have been created through dynamic interactions between clinicians and clients, tying the skills to the philosophy and precepts of DBT, and relating DBT skills to existing evidence-based practices and what the research says works.

On the following pages are a variety of DBT skills. These are not the only skills that can be used when teaching clients. Clinicians can find additional skills in other texts, on the Internet, and in professional articles. Clinicians can also create their own skills. One framework for creating your own skills would be:

- Determine which module you are developing skills for.
- Take into consideration cultural values, developmental milestones, and clients' worldview.
- Outline how the skill will facilitate balanced dialectics.
- Make it relevant to your clients.
- Appeal to visual, auditory, and kinesthetic learners.
- Be responsive to client attention span.
- Utilize multiple media.
- Make learning fun, interesting, creative, and relevant.
- Learn from the wisdom of your clients.
- On the following pages is the DBT Skills Crosswalk.

Mindfulness		Distress Tolerance		Emotional Regulation		Interpersonal Effectiveness	
Skill	Source	Skill	Source	Skill	Source	Skill	Source
Be Mindful	Marra, 2004	ACCEPTS	Linehan, 1993b	ABC	Linehan, 1993b	DEAR (WO)MAN	(Moonshine, 2007) Linehan 1993b
Body Scan	Moonshine, 2007	Crisis Survival Network	Moonshine, 2007	BEHAVIOR	Marra, 2004	Broken Record	Linehan, 1993b
Describe	Linehan, 1993b	Exploring Pros & Cons	Linehan, 1993b	Build Positive Emotions	Moonshine, 2007	Ignore	Linehan, 1993b
Effectively	Linehan, 1993b	Half Smile	Linehan, 1993b	CARES	Marra, 2004	Turn the Table	Linehan, 1993b
Mindful Eating	Moonshine, 2007	IMPROVE	Linehan, 1993b	EMOTIONS	Marra, 2004	GIVE	Linehan, 1993b
Moment to Pause	Moonshine, 2007	Keeping It In Perspective	Moonshine, 2007	Exploring Emotions	Marra, 2004	FAST	Linehan, 1993b
Non-Judgmental	Linehan, 1993b	OBJECTIVES	Marra, 2004	Feeling not Acting	Moonshine, 2007	Interactions in Relationships	Spradlin, 2003
Observe	Linehan, 1993b	Observe Breathing	Linehan, 1993b	Getting to Know Emotions	Marra, 2004	Relationship Thinking	Spradlin, 2003
ONE MIND	Marra, 2004	Radical Acceptance	Linehan, 1993b	Lemonade	Moonshine, 2007	Relationship Assumptions	Spradlin, 2003
One-Mindfully	Linehan, 1993b	Self Soothe	Linehan, 1993b	Love Dandelions	Moonshine, 2007	Rel. Mindfulness	Spradlin, 2003
Participate	Linehan, 1993b	Self Soothe First Aid Kit	Linehan, 1993b	MEDDSS	Linehan, 1993b	Dealing with Difficult People	Spradlin, 2003
Square Breathing	Moonshine, 2007	SPECIFIC PATHS	Marra, 2004	Opposite to Emotions	Linehan, 1993b	The Most Difficult	Spradlin, 2003
Turtling	Moonshine, 2007	Turning the Mind	Linehan, 1993b	Ride the Wave	Moonshine, 2007	Repairs	Spradlin, 2003
Wise Mind	Linehan, 1993b	Willingness	Linehan, 1993b	TRUST	Marra, 2004	4 Horsemen	Spradlin, 2003

MINDFULNESS

Classic

Observe	Have the clients notice what is going on around and inside themselves. Just notice. Become aware of things in this one moment.
Describe	Have clients put their observations into concrete, specific terms, while being as nonjudgmental as possible. Clients can describe a thing non-judgmentally by saying that it is unacceptable, that they don't like it, that it is painful, or that they hate it. Judgmental descriptions would assign value to themselves or others. Examples: That person is an idiot, I am terrible and deserve to be in pain, or it's hopeless, I will never be good enough.
Participate	By observing what is going on inside and around them and describing things concretely, clients are able to fully participate in their lives in a mindful way. They can participate completely in each activity they engage in.
Non-Judgmental	• Suspending evaluations about self and others. • Judging behavior as right or wrong, good or bad, but not judging the person engaging in the behavior. Behavior can generate natural and logical consequences, but we don't label the person engaging in it. • Describing things concretely. • Liking or disliking things. • Holding values that are beliefs or ethics, not judgments.
One-Mindfully	Teach clients to do one thing at a time. Each activity or behavior in which they engage needs to be done mindfully, and then they can move onto to the next activity or behavior, still dedicating themselves to each thing individually at a time. For some clients this may mean slowing down, which may be more effective than the pace at which they are living. Other clients may be able to live a fast-paced life while being one-mindful.
Effectively	• Working with clients to be as effective as possible in their lives. • Helping them to see what is more effective and avoid less effective strategies and behaviors. • Avoid judgmental words such as better, worse, good, or bad.
Wise Mind	Balancing Rational Mind and Emotional Mind to create Wise Mind. Clients are able to be more mindful and effective when they use both Rational and Emotional Mind. Be sure that clients aren't judging Rational Mind as good and Emotional Mind as bad. By being in Wise Mind, clients are in balance and have all their senses, ways of knowing, and skills at their disposal to manage their lives effectively and to act in their own best interest.

MINDFULNESS

Innovative

Moment to Pause This skill teaches clients to take a quick moment to check in with themselves on the inside, in their environment, and their interactions. By being grounded inside and around themselves they are able to make decisions and behave in ways that are in their best interest.

By taking a moment to pause, clients can stop a destructive or problematic behavior and replace it with a DBT skill. This is a simple but essential skill in reaching the goal of building a life worth living.

Square Breathing When clients take a few deep breaths it creates a moment to pause. It also results in getting more oxygen to their muscles and brains, so they may feel a bit less tense and think a bit more clearly. It also provides another opportunity for the client to disengage from destructive or problematic behavior and utilize another skill.

1. Breathe in while counting to four.
2. Hold it for four seconds.
3. Then exhale while counting to four.
4. Repeat four times.

Mindful Eating This exercise is about being fully present in the ritual of eating. It asks clients to experience the complexity and richness of eating. Clients may find themselves eating at their desk at work, in the car, or in front of the TV. While this may serve a purpose, ask them to find 3–4 times a week to eat mindfully.

Eating mindfully requires that the clients focus just on eating. They use their senses to appreciate the food. They chew each bite fully. By doing so, they will eat less food in the 15–20 minutes it takes to feel full. While being mindful, hopefully they will notice the sensation of fullness and satiation. Chewing each bite fully also produces more saliva which is one of the most effective enzymes in digestion, enabling food to be digested more completely.

ONE MIND <u>O</u>ne thing at a time

<u>N</u>ow, be in the here and now

<u>E</u>nvironment, grounded in it

<u>M</u>oment, be present in this one moment

<u>I</u>ncrease senses to be firmly in the here and now

<u>N</u>on-Judgmental of self and others

<u>D</u>escribe things in concrete, specific terms

This acronym helps clients stay present in the moment inside and around them.

MINDFULNESS

Innovative

Body Scan	Taking a few moments, have clients focus on their bodies. Clients can do this with their eyes closed or open. They can do it almost anywhere and several times a day. This exercise brings the client into the here and now and may also put their pain in perspective by making space for comfort and neutral sensations. Provide instructions to the clients by first asking clients to go inside themselves. Here are some suggested instructions to give to clients.

- Notice any pain, discomfort, and tension you are feeling
- Just notice it, don't do anything about it
- Notice relaxation, comfort, and feeling at ease
- Also become aware of neutral sensations
- Take another moment to be with yourself on the inside
- Now become aware of yourself on the outside
- Notice your feet on the ground
- Become of aware of the environment with all five of your senses
- Lighting, temperature, sound, perhaps smell and taste
- Become of aware of people around you, closeness and distance. Even if they are in another room or building, image their proximity
- One more moment on the outside, the inside and come back

Be Mindful	This skill asks clients to be mindful of one or two things. The client pays attention to practicing a specific skill or staying in the moment. Ask clients to Be Mindful of self care, having healthy fun, and connection to support system.

Turtling	Clients use a variety of strategies to take care of themselves, just like turtles.

- Retreating inside themselves and then reemerging when it is safe.
- Going slowly and methodically, being thoughtful about how to invest time, energy, and attention.
- Using their hard outer shells to let things roll off their backs. This is a great way to deflect the judgments of others.
- Being adaptive; turtles are able to live in water and on land.
- Persistently self-righting. When turtles get turned over, they use their weight and environment to get themselves right-side up and back in balance. It may take a few hours or even a couple of days, but when life turns turtles upside down, they work hard to right themselves and get back in balance.
- Although they aren't aggressive animals, turtles will protect themselves when absolutely necessary through snapping or biting.

Turtles are very important symbols in many cultures or communities such as Native American and Hindu. Turtling will also resonate with kids and teenagers, because of Teenage Mutant Ninja Turtles.

DISTRESS TOLERANCE

Classic

Exploring Pros & Cons

This skill explores:

- Pros of having crisis
- Cons of not having crisis
- Pros of not having crisis
- Cons of having crisis

Pros of having Crisis or Stress	Cons of not having Crisis or Stress
Cons of having Crisis or Stress	Pros of not having Crisis or Stress

Most of us would put an emphasis on the last two, but it is enormously helpful to explore the first two.

What does the client get out of having crises?

- Extra attention
- Held less responsible
- Adrenaline rush
- Scaring others

Help the client meet their needs in a more direct, effective way so they don't need crises.

What are the downsides to not having crises?

- It's boring
- Having to do all those mundane things like clean the house
- Less support from family and friends
- Accepting full responsibility

Assist the client in building the skills to successfully balance responsibility, chores, and expectations with fun, enjoyment, and relationships.

Self Soothe

Have the clients self-soothe with all five of their senses: sight, sound, smell, taste, and touch. The caveat of this skill is that if they overly self-soothe with a particular sense then they skip that sense. For example if the client overeats, then taste is not the sense to self-soothe with.

DISTRESS TOLERANCE

Classic

Turning the Mind This one teaches clients that they are in the driver's seat with their mind. This includes thoughts, feelings, impulses, and even behavior.

Clients can identify which road they are driving on. They can choose to stay on the same road or they can make a left turn changing their thoughts, feelings, impulses, or behavior. They can make a right turn which would take their thoughts, feelings, impulses, or behaviors in a different direction. They can also make a U-turn and start over. It is also possible for clients to stop driving for a while and take a break.

Observe Breathing This exercise orients client to their breath. Ask clients to spend a few moments paying attention to their breath. One way this is helpful is as a distraction from the crisis or stressful situation. It also can have a calming effect by providing more oxygen to the mind and body, reducing anxiety or distressing bodily sensations. Here are some ways you can direct clients to use this skill:

- Inhale while counting to 5 slowly
- Let the breath out will counting to 5 slowly
- Repeat 5 times

- Take a deep breath while taking one long stride
- Let out the breath while taking one long stride
- Repeat 3 times

- Take long slow breaths in and out while imagining relaxing on a beach or at home under the covers. Do this for 90 seconds.

- For every distressing thought or painful sensation complete a full deep breath in and out.

Willingness Willingness exercises are helpful in the middle of a crisis. Clients can practice willingness to accept reality, a bad day, things not going their way, or to accept that they can't control others and the world around them. Willingness is open and accepting. It is life-enhancing, energy generating and relationship enhancing. By comparison, willfulness is acting like a 2 year old. Wanting what we want even when it isn't in our best interest or does us harm. Willfulness is exhausting, harms relationships, and reduces quality of life.

DISTRESS TOLERANCE

Classic

ACCEPTS	<u>H</u>ave clients distract themselves with: <u>A</u>ctivities <u>C</u>ompassion <u>C</u>hoices <u>E</u>motions <u>P</u>ushing Away <u>T</u>houghts <u>S</u>ensations
IMPROVE	This acronym provides a series of things for the clients to focus on that will distract them from a crisis or stressful situation. Clients can take their time with this one, which will give their nervous system time to settle down. <u>I</u>magery <u>M</u>eaning <u>P</u>rayer <u>R</u>elaxation <u>O</u>ne-Mindfully <u>V</u>acation <u>E</u>ncouragement
Half Smile	Have the clients find something in their day or in their lives that can give them a genuine half-smile. It can be: • A good cup of coffee • Blue sky • Payday • A long weekend coming up • A pleasant memory • The joy on child's face When a client has a half-smile, they are a bit more relaxed in their face, neck, and shoulders. People respond differently to someone with a smile than to someone who is angry or upset. If the client is treated nicely because they are smiling that might improve their day a little bit more.
Radical Acceptance	• The Serenity Prayer • Clients can control themselves in terms of their thoughts, feelings and actions. • Clients don't have control over what happens around them or what others do. • The clients effectively focus their attention and energy on what they can control and change: themselves.

DISTRESS TOLERANCE

Innovative

Crisis Survival Network	It is important for everyone to have a crisis survival network. Hopefully your clients have one and you are not the only one on it. Educate your clients about who is helpful to have on their list and people who make things worse. Having as many people as possible on the list, and using them flexibly, are key to making this skill most useful.
Keeping It In Perspective	Ask the clients if this is the worst crisis they have ever had to deal with. Typically they will answer this affirmatively. If so, you create a metaphor that this is the marathon of crises and all of their other crises and difficulties have been in training. The clients are now in the best shape of their lives. They are well experienced and they can definitely deal with this crisis effectively.
Self Soothe First Aid Kit	This one can be quite creative. The client puts together a kit that is self soothing. It can be on their computer, in their purse/wallet, or desk drawer. It can be a box that they decorate and fill with things that are soothing for them. Things in the self soothe 1st Aid Kit have to be effective and not harmful in any way. An alternative way to talk about this skill is to call it a tool kit, not a 1st aid kit.
OBJECTIVES	Clients can use this acronym to effectively deal with difficult experiences.

1. **O**ne thing at a time
2. **B**e effective
3. Avoid **J**udgments
4. Cope with **E**motions
5. Consider **C**onsequences
6. Take **T**ime
7. Use **I**ntrospection
8. Act consistently with **V**alues
9. Focus on desired **E**ndings
10. Balance **S**hort-term and long-term goals

SPECIFIC PATHS	This acronym helps clients stay on path to build the life they want for themselves.

1. What is my **S**upreme Concern?
2. **P**ractice my skills
3. Focus my **E**nergy and **C**oncentration
4. **I** can be effective
5. Have **F**aith
6. Consider what is **I**mportant
7. Have **C**ourage and **P**atience
8. Pay **A**ttention
9. Complete **T**asks
10. Be **H**umble and have **S**ensitivity

EMOTIONAL REGULATION

Classic

ABC	Using this acronym helps clients to achieve balance in the face of difficult situations. When the client is having a bad day or something unpleasant occurs, they can use this skill to remind themselves of positive things they are good at and use strategies that they have prepared for just such occasions. **A**ccumulate Positives **B**uild Mastery **C**ope Ahead
MEDDSS	This skill is all about self-care. Self-care dramatically enhances our emotional well being: **M**astery **E**xercise **D**iet **D**rugs (Take prescription drugs as directed but not illicit ones) **S**leep **S**pirituality
Love Dandelions	This skill provides clients with the opportunity to accept themselves or to love their shadow selves. Clients build an awareness and acceptance of parts of themselves that they dislike or find unattractive. There are some things they can't change about themselves, but by being aware of them they can minimize damage and distress.
Opposite to Emotions	First ask the client what emotion they have a lot of that is problematic or troublesome. Ask the clients to be mindfully present with the strong emotions, but not act on them. Ask the clients to identify the opposite emotion to the strong emotion. Then ask the client when they notice the opposite emotion. Have the client identify 4–6 things that they can do on any given day that brings the opposite emotion into their awareness. After this has been established, give the client the assignment that whenever they are feeling the strong emotion, to hold it in their awareness and actively engage in activities that bring the opposite emotion to their awareness as well.

EMOTIONAL REGULATION

Innovative

Lemonade out of Lemons	This skill is about having clients refocus their weaknesses and problematic thinking and behavior into strengths.
	This happens when a client takes the skills and strengths they do have, but may be using in a way that causes harm or problems in their lives. They can take these skills and strengths and focus them differently in their lives.
	For example, an identity thief who becomes a security expert; a car thief who works with police and insurance companies to reduce auto theft; the drug addict who gets into recovery and becomes an addictions counselor.
	With this skill, clients learn they don't have to start over. They learn that while some changes may be required, they don't have to be overwhelmed with trying to be completely different.
Feeling not Acting	Feeling a strong impulse or emotion is not the same as acting on it. This would be two steps. Clients can use their Moment to Pause to identify and feel an impulse or urge. They can choose to engage in the impulse, use a skill to manage it, or tolerate it while doing nothing.
Ride the Wave	This skill uses the metaphor that the tide comes and goes, but it is always with us just like our emotions and strong impulses. Some days are stormy and chaotic while other days are calmer.
	While it might feel like a particular emotional state might last forever or that this is the last feeling the client will ever have, it will eventually shift and change into the next emotion.
	A visualization or artwork exercise could be useful. Direct the client to imagine that they are riding the wave of their emotions. This can be done with surfing, snowboarding, skiing, or skateboarding. It is a lot more fun to do this when it's intense than when it's calm. And to do it well, the client has to be fully in the moment. This skill seems to resonate with teenagers and young adults.

EMOTIONAL REGULATION

Innovative

Build Positive Emotions

The client can balance out negative emotions and experiences by increasing positive emotions and experiences.

<u>Short Term</u>: Do pleasant things that are possible now.

<u>Long term</u>: Make changes in your life so that positive events will occur more often. Build a "life worth living."

1. <u>Work toward goals</u>:
   - Make a list of positive events you want.
   - List small steps toward goals.
   - Take the first step.

2. <u>Attend to relationships</u>:
   - Repair old relationships.
   - Reach out for new relationships.
   - Work on current relationships.

3. <u>Avoid avoiding</u>:
   - Avoid giving up.
   - Effectively and actively problem solve.
   - Do things that are necessary.

Getting to Know Emotions

Have the client explore the following process:

Environmental precipitants. Determine what happened in the environment just prior to your current emotional state.

Identify emotions. Identify and describe your emotions.

Experience in the body. Identify and describe bodily experience of emotions.

Cognitions related to the emotions. Identify and describe the thoughts you are having about your emotions.

Behavior. Identify the behavior that you have engaged in, or have urges to engage in, as a result of your emotional state.

Aftermath. Explore the aftermath of the situation. How did you feel? What happened? What were the positive and negative consequences? What went well? What have you learned? What might you do differently next time?

EMOTIONAL REGULATION

Innovative

Exploring Your Emotions

Assumptions. What assumptions are you making about your feelings, yourself, others, and the world around you?

Counteracting the assumption. How can you counteract or ignore these assumptions?

Notice change in emotion. Identify and describe how your emotional state changes.

Non-judgmental. Apply your non-judgmental skills, both for you and others.

Future Tripping. Evaluate if you are future-tripping; identify and describe.

Challenge tripping. How can you challenge or ignore future-tripping.

One-mindful. Be mindful; be completely present in this one moment.

Meaning about me. What meaning does this emotional state have to you?

Challenge the meaning. Contrast or challenge this meaning to you. Think about how this might be related to the earlier assumption.

Non-judgmental. Once again, apply your non-judgmental skills to yourself and others.

Change Body. Change your posture and energy level. Notice change in emotional state.

Facial Expression. Change your facial expression. Notice change in emotional state.

Change Behaviors. Change your behaviors and activities. Notice change in emotional state.

EMOTIONAL REGULATION

Innovative

CARES   This acronym is short, making it easy to remember. This skill will be useful for clients who need to modulate their arousal response.

Calm, coached practice

Arousal monitoring

Relaxation and rest

Emotions in the environment

Sleep an effective amount

TRUST   This acronym is short, which makes it easy to remember. The client who will benefit from this skill comes across as scary or intimidating without being aware of it.

Trust yourself.

Redirect impulses and urges

Use your skills to be effective

Seen, act consistently on how you want others to see you.

Tame your emotions and reactions

EMOTIONS   This acronym is concrete and straightforward which is useful for some clients.

Exposure to emotions

Mindful of current emotions

Outline a plan to deal with emotions

Take opposite action

Increase positive experiences

Obstacles and plan to overcome them

Notice what is going on

Support system

BEHAVIOR   This is another acronym. This one is useful for clients who want to focus on healing versus hurting behavior or those who are strongly connected with a value system.

Use effective **B**ehavior

Be grounded in the **E**nvironment

Do things that are **H**ealing not Hurting

Act in my best interest

Be consistent with my **V**alues

Imagine getting through difficulties

Focus on the desired **O**utcome

Reinforce my successes

If the client doesn't like a particular letter, they can change it to something else as long as it is effective in being prosocial and well-adjusted.

INTERPERSONAL EFFECTIVENESS

Classic

Broken Record	The client practices being a broken record with themselves. They keep coming back to their needs and wants.
Ignore	Ignore self-judgments and judgments of others
Turn the Tables	Be reciprocal. Do things for other people.
GIVE	This skill is designed to provide the clients with capacities to improve and sustain relationships in healthy ways. **G**entle in relationships **I**nterest in others **V**alidate **E**asy Manner
FAST	Self-respect is the goal of this skill. This skill helps clients who are out of balance with codependency or focus on others to also focus on themselves. **F**air to self **A**pologize less **S**tick to values **T**ruthful with self
DEAR WOMAN or MAN	This skill is used to accomplish a task or meet an objective. Based on the client's gender I teach them either WOMAN or MAN. **D**escribe what is wanted **E**ncourage others to help **A**sk for what is wanted **R**einforce others **W**illingness **O**bserve **M**indful **A**ppear Confident **N**egotiate

INTERPERSONAL EFFECTIVENESS

Innovative

Relationship Thinking	This skill is about couples and families using dialectical thinking rather than dichotomous thinking.

Dichotomous thinking to avoid:

- Always
- Never
- All or nothing
- Black or white
- This or that
- With me or against me

Dialectical thinking to increase:

- Both/and
- Positive and negative feelings
- Thoughts and feelings
- Shades of gray
- Needs and wants
- Self and others
- Talking and listening
- Balance

Relationship Assumptions	This skill puts the dialectical philosophy into couples' or families' language.

1. Both of us are doing the best we can
2. Both of us can be more effective
3. Both of us want to be more effective
4. Both of have to be more effective, try harder, and apply our skills
5. Neither of us caused all of the problems in our relationship, and we both have to work together to solve them

INTERPERSONAL EFFECTIVENESS

Innovative

Relationship Mindfulness	Clients can apply mindfulness to their relationships: • Identify generalizations • Describe assumptions • Suspend judgments • Avoid jumping to conclusions • Empower self, don't defeat self • Use One-Mindfulness • Be non-judgmental • Participate effectively
Interactions in Relationships	This skill helps clients to be in the moment and to interact effectively with family, friends, and others. Below is a list steps that clients can use: • Observe and Describe the interaction • Be Mindful of emotions • Engage in opposite behaviors when useful • Remember to breathe • Take a Non-Judgmental stance • Use assertive communication • Show self-respect and respect for others • Develop frustration tolerance By using this skill clients will experience improved communication, interactions, and more ability to sustain relationships in a variety of contexts.
Dealing with Difficult People	• Describe your relationship • Describe quality of relationship • Explore your particular sensitivity to this relationship • Participate in improving this relationship • Identify and overcome obstacles to improvement
The Most Difficult	Rate the difficulty, identify feelings, minimize judgments, and engage in effective interactions.

INTERPERSONAL EFFECTIVENESS

Innovative

Repairs	Many clients probably grew up, or are currently growing up, in families that didn't teach them how to make healthy repairs. Making repairs is about taking responsibility, apologizing when appropriate, accepting an apology when it makes sense, having the ability to let go and move on, and learning from the situation to avoid it in the future
Four Horsemen of the Apocalypse	This uses the metaphor of the Four Horsemen said to appear at the end of the world. If a client has the Four Horsemen in his or her relationships, then the relationship might be over. Criticism, contempt, defensiveness, and stonewalling may be the four most destructive behaviors in relationships. The above Horsemen may not apply to these clients. Each client can identify their own Horsemen and then implement strategies to keep these destructive forces out of their relationships. Other Horsemen can be:

Youth	*Adults*
• Not communicating	• Dishonesty
• Withdrawal	• Not taking MH meds
• Dishonesty	• Out-of-control spending
• School refusal	• Credit card debt
• Playing video games	• Workaholism
• Bullying	• Drugs and alcohol
• Violence	• Violence
• Drugs & alcohol	• Infidelity
• Delinquency	• Internet sex/pornography

CHAPTER 3
General DBT Handouts

What is DBT?

Dialectical Behavior Therapy (DBT) is about learning tools and skills to empower you to be as effective as you can be in your life.

These tools and skills can be used nearly every day, in most situations, and in a variety of relationships.

Over the coming weeks and months, you will learn a lot of new things. This will require you to practice in session and complete homework assignments.

Like most things worth learning, it takes time, energy, and commitment. While learning DBT you will experience moments of humor, creativity, and relevancy to your life.

D.B.T. in Life™

What are dialectics?

Dialectics are the art of holding 2 or more things in balance that are in conflict, contrary, or mismatched and yet they are both real or true. It is about synthesizing things that seem to be in opposition. Dialectics are the kernel of truth in each person's perspective in an argument or dialogue. Dialectics are all the ironies and paradoxes in life. Being dialectical is about balancing competing needs. Below are some dialectics you can benefit from keeping in balance.

Wants and needs
Feelings and thoughts
Problems and solutions
Contemplation and action
Recreation and responsibilities
Being right and making mistakes
Self-interest and interest in others
Skill enhancement and self-acceptance
Doing things alone and being able to ask for help

D.B.T. in Life™

Some Days Nothing Goes Well

D.B.T. teaches you many skills. It encourages balance. It provides you with the tools to be in the here and now, to regulate emotions, tolerate distress, and have effective relationships. Even with all of these tools and skills, there are days that nothing goes well.

Some days and in some situations, you can use all of the tools you have acquired from DBT and find you still can't be effective. No matter how hard you work or how committed you are to DBT, others and the environment will be too powerful. There will be times when you need to accept that you are unable to get your needs met or avoid a negative outcome. Life is still unfair every now and then.

At these times, you may be tempted to give up or throw away your progress. You may have an impulse to revert to old, problematic behavior, have impulses to harm yourself, or a desire to damage your relationships. It is essential when having these experiences that you use damage control, patience, and hold a long-term perspective.

D.B.T. in Life™

Some Days Nothing Goes Well

Ways I can identify when the interaction or situation is out of my control:

_____

_____

Strategies I can use for damage control:

_____

_____

Ways that I can be patient:

_____

_____

Strategies that I can use to maintain a long-term perspective:

_____

_____

Ways I can stay the course with DBT even when it doesn't seem to be working:

_____

_____

_____

_____

D.B.T. in Life™

D.B.T. in Life™

Sunday	Monday	Tuesday	Wednesday	Thursday	Friday	Saturday
	Notes:					

Use this calendar month template to document when you use DBT skills. Put a sticker or star on each day that you use at least one skill. If you like, you can also list the skills that you used that day. By tracking if you use at least one skill a day, you will use the skills a lot more often.

D.B.T. in Life™

	Sunday	Monday	Tuesday	Wednesday	Thursday	Friday	Saturday
Notes:							

Why is balance important?

Balance is holding many things at once without getting knocked down. Things that can knock you down are situations, relationships, and life in general. With DBT you are holding many things in balance to be effective with yourself, others, and in a variety of situations. Balance is about not being too much to one side or the other. Balance is different for different people in different situations. Balance is imperfect. Gymnasts on the balance beam can be a bit to one side or the other or leaning a bit forward or backward, but still be in balance.

Being in balance is an effective way to accomplish tasks, manage emotions, tolerate distress, maintain healthy relationships, and sustain self-respect. Some things to keep in mind: Sustaining balance is an essential ingredient in being dialectical.

D.B.T. in Life™

Acronyms

Acronyms are words in which each letter means something. There are many acronyms in DBT because they are easy to learn and remember. Also, they may have repetition in them that adds emphasis to how important that idea is.

Not everyone cares for acronyms and yet they can be very useful in building the life you want and becoming the person you want to be. If there is a letter or letters that stand for a word or concept that doesn't fit for you, you can usually change it to another word that starts with the same letter that resonates with you more or is more on target for what you are trying to accomplish.

It is also possible to create your own DBT acronyms. Work with your clinician to design acronyms that will work for you.

Use your acronyms by going through each letter and engaging in the activity or process that each letter stands for. An example is MEDDSS. MEDDSS is practiced on a daily basis. You can engage in things that you have Mastery over, a little bit of Exercise and movement, eat a balanced Diet, take prescription Drugs as directed, get a healthy amount of Sleep and have sense of Spirituality and meaning in your life every day.

Mindfulness Acronym

O = Q̲ne Thing at a Time
N = Be in the N̲ow
E = Be Grounded in the E̲nvironment

M = Be M̲indfully Present in the Moment
I = I̲ncrease Senses
N = Use my N̲on-Judgmental Skills
D = D̲escribe What is Going On

Distress Tolerance Acronyms

O = One thing at a time
B = Be effective
J = Avoid Judgments
E = Cope with Emotions
C = Consider Consequences
T = Take Time
I = Use Introspection
V = Act consistently with Values
E = Focus on desired Endings
S = Balance Short-term and long-term goals

S = What is my Supreme Concern?
P = Practice my skills
E = Focus my Energy
C = Use Concentration
I = I can be effective
F = Have Faith
I = Figure out what is Important
C = Have Courage

P = Be Patient
A = Pay Attention
T = Complete Tasks
H = Be Humble
S = Have Sensitivity

A = Activities
C = Compassion
C = Choices
E = Emotions
P = Pushing Away
T = Thoughts
S = Sensations

I = Imagery
M = Meaning
P = Prayer
R = Relaxation
O = One-Mindfully
V = Vacation
E = Encouragement

D.B.T. in Life™

Emotional Regulation Acronyms

M = Mastery
E = Exercise
D = Diet
D = Drugs (Medication)
S = Sleep
S = Spirituality

T = Trust myself
R = Redirect my impulses and urges
U = Use my skills
S = Act how I want others to See me
T = Tame my emotions and impulses

B = Use effective Behavior
E = Be grounded in the Environment
H = Do Healing not hurting things
A = Act in my best interests
V = Be consistent with my Values
I = Imagine getting through it
O = Focus on the desired Outcome
R = Reinforce my successes

A = Accumulate Positives
B = Build Mastery
C = Cope Ahead

E = Exposure to emotions
M = Mindful of current emotions
O = Outline a plan to deal with emotions
T = Take opposite action
I = Increase positive experiences
O = Obstacles and plan to overcome
N = Notice what is going on
S = Support system

C = Being Calm
A = Monitoring Arousal
R = Finding rest and Relaxation
E = Effectively coping with my Emotions
S = Getting a healthy amount of Sleep

Interpersonal Effectiveness Acronyms

G = Gentle in relationships
I = Interest in others
V = Validate
E = Easy Manner

F = Fair to self
A = Apologize less
S = Stick to values
T = Truthful with self

D = Describe what is wanted
E = Encourage others to help
A = Ask for what is wanted
R = Reinforce others

W = Willingness to tolerate not always getting it my way
O = Observe what is going on inside and around me
M = Mindfully present in the current moment
A = Appear confident
N = Negotiate with others

Building a Life Worth Living

DBT is about building a life worth living. A life worth living is about having the best life you can have. It is about having a full life that sustains you psychologically, emotionally, and interpersonally.

My Life Worth Living would look like:

_____

_____

_____

_____

Things in my life that get in the way of building a Life Worth Living:

_____

_____

Ways I can minimize or eliminate these things:

_____

_____

Things in my life that support a Life Worth Living:

_____

_____

Ways I can do more things that build a Life Worth Living:

_____

_____

D.B.T. in Life™

Recovery & Resiliency

Recovery is about living optimally and reaching your potential. Being in recovery can be about being substance free if you have an addiction; however, recovery is more than just abstinence. Recovery is about living beyond your problems. It is a strength-based perspective that empowers you to build the life you strive for. It is about being resilient and bouncing back from difficulties and problems. Recovery is something that is practiced every day. It is imperfect and forgiving.

Examples of recovery and resiliency in my life already:

_____

_____

Barriers and obstacles to recovery and resiliency in my life:

_____

_____

Strategies I can use to overcome these barriers and obstacles:

_____

_____

Ways I can increase my recovery and resiliency in my life:

_____

_____

D.B.T. in Life™

Barriers & Obstacles

Barriers and obstacles are things that get in the way of using the DBT skills in your life. Doing something new, like the skills, usually doesn't work perfectly the first few times. There will be situations when you can't use the skills or don't remember to do so. To get the most out of the skills it will take lots of practice, particularly at times before you really need it. To be the most effective in this process it will be useful to anticipate potential barriers and obstacles and how you will deal with them so that you can use the skills effectively.

Some of potential barriers and obstacles are:

_____

_____

_____

I can deal with these barriers and obstacles by:

_____

_____

_____

Skills I can use even when I can't resolve the barriers and obstacles:

_____

_____

_____

D.B.T. in Life™

Therapy-Interfering Behaviors

Therapy interfering behaviors are thoughts and behaviors that get in the way of the therapeutic process. Sometimes these are intentional and sometimes they are not. You may have an awareness of when you are engaging in therapy-interfering behaviors and there may be times when you aren't aware. Therapy-interfering behaviors may be an expression of your anxiety, shame, guilt, fear, pain, and other uncomfortable feelings. There is no reason to judge yourself for the therapy-interfering behaviors; however, you need to reduce and eliminate these behaviors to the best of your ability.

Some of my therapy-interfering behaviors may look like:

_____

_____

_____

Strategies I can use to minimize or eliminate my therapy-interfering behaviors:

_____

_____

_____

Ways my therapist and others can help me eliminate or minimize therapy-interfering behaviors:

_____

_____

_____

D.B.T. in Life™

Skills Modules

DBT teaches skills in 4 categories:

Mindfulness: Being in the current moment, today, or the here and now most of the time. It is about being non-judgmental with yourself and others.

Distress Tolerance: Managing frustrations, stress, and problems effectively. It is about being active in solving problems and accepting when things are out of your control.

Emotional Regulation: Having healthy emotional expression and impulse control. Balancing coping and managing emotions as well as tolerating them by "riding the wave."

Interpersonal Effectiveness: Getting your needs met in relationships. Sustain healthy relationships while also maintaining self-respect.

One or all of the DBT skills categories will be helpful to me by:

_____

_____

_____

_____

_____

_____

_____

_____

D.B.T. in Life™

Pros & Cons

Pros of Staying the Same	Cons of Engaging in DBT

Cons of Staying the Same	Pros of Engaging in DBT

Pros & Cons

Pros of Not Using DBT Skills	Cons of Using DBT Skills
Cons of Not Using DBT Skills	Pros of Using DBT Skills

Pros & Cons

Pros of No Homework	Cons of Completing Homework

Cons of No Homework	Pros of Completing Homework

D.B.T. in Life™

Pros & Cons

Pros of Not Using Diary Cards	Cons of Using Diary Cards
Cons of Not Using Diary Cards	Pros of Using Diary Cards

Pros & Cons

The Therapy-Interfering Behavior I am exploring is:

_____

Pros of My Therapy-Interfering Behavior	Cons of Stopping My Therapy-Interfering Behavior
Cons of **My Therapy-Interfering Behavior**	**Pros of Stopping** **My Therapy-Interfering Behavior**

D.B.T. in Life™

Cost-Benefits Analysis

Issue I am analyzing:

_____

Benefits of	Costs of
Costs of	Benefits of

D.B.T. in Life™

Positive & Negatives

Issue I am analyzing:

_____

Positive of	Negatives of
Negatives of	Positive of

D.B.T. in Life™

Diary Card

DBT Skills	Mon	Tue	Wed	Thur	Fri	Sat	Sun	Total
Mindfulness								
Distress Tolerance								
Emotional Regulation								
Interpersonal Effectiveness								

Comments:

D.B.T. in Life™

Diary Card, Part II

	Mon	Tue	Wed	Thur	Fri	Sat	Sun
Impulses To*							
Feelings*							
Behaviors*							
DBT Skills**							

Rating Scale: 0-5*	** Rate DBT Skills
Impulses To	0 = Not thought about or used
Feelings	1 = Thought about, didn't want to use skill
Behaviors	2 = Thought about, didn't use, but wanted to
	3 = Tried to use skill, couldn't use it
*5 is the highest	4 = Tried to use skill, didn't help
	5 = Used skill, it helped

Comments:

D.B.T. in Life™

63

Simple Chain Analysis

What problem behavior am I analyzing?

_____

Let's look at the chain of events that resulted in the problem behavior.

```
( Vulnerability )  ( Triggers )  ( Problem )
(     Link      )  (   Link   )  ( Behavior Link )
```

Vulnerability Link: In what ways was I vulnerable?
May be internal, such as thoughts, judgments, feelings, and/or impulses.
May be environmental, such as events, person, places, and/or situations.
May be interpersonal, such as difficult interactions with family and/or friends.

```
[                                          ]
```

Triggers Link: What were the internal, environmental, and interpersonal triggers?
May be my actions, thoughts, feelings, impulses, events, people, or places.

```
[                                          ]
```

Problem Behavior Link: What was the problem behavior and any related behaviors?
These are behavioral expressions that are problematic, harmful, or destructive.

```
[                                          ]
```

Solution Opportunities

Now it is time to explore each link to come up with more effective response strategies.

Vulnerability Link: _____

Solution #1: _____

Solution #2: _____

Solution #3: _____

Triggers Link: _____

Solution #1: _____

Solution #2: _____

Solution #3: _____

Problem Behavior Link: _____

Solution #1: _____

Solution #2: _____

Solution #3: _____

In-Depth Chain Analysis

What problem behavior am I analyzing?

_____

Let's look at the chain of events that resulted in the problem behavior.

Vulnerability Link: In what ways was I vulnerable?
May be internal, such as thoughts, judgments, feelings, and/or impulses.
May be environmental, such as events, person, places, and/or situations.
May be interpersonal, such as difficult interactions with family and/or friends.

[ ]

Connecting Links: What connected my vulnerability and triggers?
May be my actions, thoughts, feelings, impulses, events, people, or places.

[ ]

In-Depth Chain Analysis, Part II

Triggers Link: What were the internal, environmental, and interpersonal triggers? May be my actions, thoughts, feelings, impulses, events, people, or places.

Connecting Links: What connected my triggers with the problem behavior? May be my actions, thoughts, feelings, impulses, events, people, or places.

Problem Behavior Link: What was the problem behavior and any related behaviors? These are behavioral expressions that are problematic, harmful, or destructive.

D.B.T. in Life™

Solution Opportunities

Explore each link to come up with more effective response strategies.

Vulnerability Link: _____

Solution #1: _____

Solution #2: _____

Solution #3: _____

Connecting Link: _____

Solution #1: _____

Solution #2: _____

Solution #3: _____

Triggers Link: _____

Solution #1: _____

Solution #2: _____

Solution #3: _____

Connecting Link: _____

Solution #1: _____

Solution #2: _____

Solution #3: _____

Problem Behavior Link: _____

Solution #1: _____

Solution #2: _____

Solution #3: _____

D.B.T. in Life™

Preventing Relapses

Problems and difficulties can come back sometimes, so it is useful to figure out what your warning signs might be and how you proactively deal with them before they become full-blown problems:

Warning Sign: _____

DBT Skill: _____

Desired Outcome: _____

Warning Sign: _____

DBT Skill: _____

Desired Outcome: _____

Warning Sign: _____

DBT Skill: _____

Desired Outcome: _____

If warning sign continues or worsens, contact support system or a helping professional.

D.B.T. in Life™

Recovery Plan

Recovery is about being the best possible person. It is about reaching your potential while dealing with difficulties, stress, and problems. Recovery is about effectively dealing with mental health and substance use problems. It also entails effectively dealing with family and support system, job, meaningful activities, recreational opportunities and having fun, just to name a few. The next few pages provide an opportunity to develop a recovery plan which can then be implemented.

This is my plan for recovery and optimal functioning:

My life in recovery looks like:

_____

_____

_____

_____

Which DBT Skills are most helpful for me?

_____

_____

_____

_____

Recovery Plan

1. Practicing MEDDSS daily establishes a healthy self-care regimen.

a. Exercise

_____

_____

b. Diet: Balanced and nutritious

_____

_____

c. Drugs: Prescribed medication as directed and don't use illicit drugs

_____

_____

d. Sleeping: a healthy amount

_____

_____

Page 2 of 6

Recovery Plan

2. Prevention of Relapse or Return to Old Problematic Behavior:

a. The most important warning signs of problems reoccurring:

_____

_____

_____

b. When I notice the warning signs, I will use the following DBT Skills:

_____

_____

_____

3. Healthy Support System:

These are the people in my support system that support my recovery and use of DBT skills:

_____

_____

_____

Recovery Plan

4. Having Fun and Recreation is an Important Part of Recovery:

a. I will ensure that I have time for fun and recreation in my life on a regular basis by using the following strategies:

_____

_____

_____

b. These are the fun and recreational activities that I will participate in on a regular basis that support my recovery:

_____

_____

_____

c. I will utilize community support meetings by:

_____

_____

_____

Page 4 of 6

Recovery Plan

5. Dealing with Stress:

a. The most stressful things in my life are:

_____

_____

_____

b. Previous ways I have effectively dealt with stress?

_____

_____

_____

c. What DBT skills will I use to manage my stress?

_____

_____

_____

D.B.T. in Life™

Recovery Plan

6. Recovery Goals:

a. What progress have I made toward my recovery?

_____

_____

_____

b. What am I currently working on in my recovery?

_____

_____

_____

c. What will I do to maintain positive changes and continue my growth?

_____

_____

_____

7. Other Things to Consider:

_____

_____

Page 6 of 6

D.B.T. in Life™

DBT Crossword Puzzle

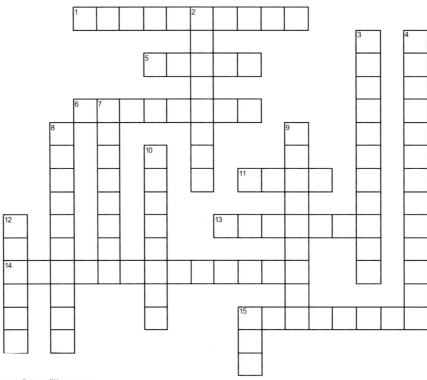

www.CrosswordWeaver.com

ACROSS

1 DBT teaches me skills for Emotional _____.

5 _____ cards are a way that I can count how many times I used my skills everyday.

6 Some of the skills are _____ which is when each letter stands for a word.

11 Acronyms are _____ to remember and emphasize what is most useful.

13 Through the use of my DBT skills I am keeping things in _____.

14 _____ Effectiveness is about having healthy relationships with myself and others.

15 _____ Tolerance helps me build frustration tolerance.

DOWN

2 Chain _____ is an exercise I use to figure out why I engaged in problematic behavior.

3 Being grounded in today.

4 Solution _____ worksheets gives me the chance to figure what skills I can use in the future.

7 I can document that I use at least one a skill every day, but putting a sticker on my _____,

8 Ironies and paradoxes are _____.

9 I can figure out some of the barriers and _____ to using DBT skills in my life.

10 My _____ plan helps me take care of myself and avoid difficulties.

12 DBT has a lot of _____ that help me build a life worth living.

15 The initials we use as a shorthand for Dialectical Behavior Therapy are?

D.B.T. in Life™

76

DBT Crossword Puzzle Answers

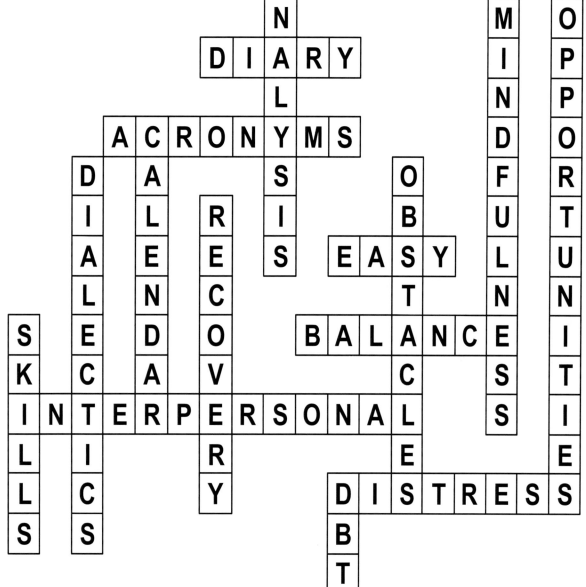

D.B.T. in Life™

D.B.T. in Life™

CHAPTER 4

Mindfulness Worksheets

Mindfulness

Mindfulness is about keeping your awareness in the current moment most of the time. It is about being present and aware in your life today. Mindfulness would say the past is the past and the future isn't here yet.

What has happened in the past has already happened. It can't be changed. It is possible to learn from the past, reflect on the past, or just have a memory of the past.

Since the future hasn't happened yet, there is no point in excessively worrying about what is to come. And yet, it is effective to plan and prepare for the future.

Being in the past and future mindfully or intentionally is optimal. If instead you live your life mind*lessly* in the past or future, you can miss out on really important things going on right now and end up regretting it later (or some other rationale).

Mindfulness would say: If you are going to spend time and energy focusing on the past and future; do it intentionally and with full awareness. However, spend most of your time in the present moment, in the here and now, in today. This allows you to fully experience your life as it is happening, rather than what it was or what it might be.

How might practicing mindfulness help you achieve your goals?

_____

_____

_____

_____

Mindfulness

How might practicing mindfulness help you act more effectively in your daily life when challenges arise?

_____

_____

_____

What is hard about practicing mindfulness:

_____

_____

Strategies to overcome what is hard about practicing mindfulness:

_____

_____

What is useful about practicing mindfulness:

_____

_____

Strategies to increase mindfulness in daily life:

_____

_____

_____

D
B
T

I
N

L
I
F
E
™

Square Breathing

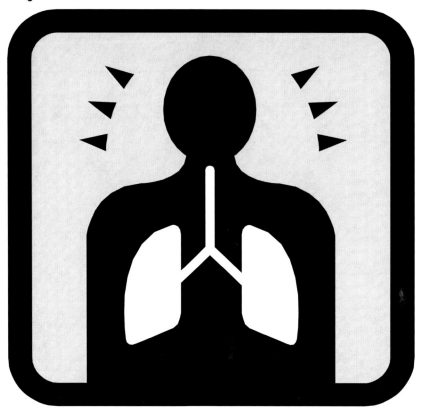

Do this skill mindfully, with full awareness, focusing only on your breathing. If you notice your mind wandering, just notice and bring yourself back to your breathing. By taking these long, slow, deep breaths, you will get more air into your lungs which will get more air to your muscles which will reduce tension and more air to your brain so you can think a little bit more clearly.

1. Breathe in while counting to 4.

2. Hold your breath while counting to 4.

3. Exhale while counting to 4.

4. Repeat 4 times.

Try "Square Breathing" at least 4 times a day.

More often if it is useful.

Observe & Describe

These two skills are about noticing what is going on inside and outside. Start by focusing on the here & now. Let go of any thoughts about the past or future. Just be present right now. If thoughts come in, notice them and then let them go as if you were watching clouds floating by.

Let's take a moment to check in on the inside and outside. An important part of this process is being non-judgmental. This means not assigning a value to yourself or others (for example, "good," "bad," "stupid," "worthless"). Stick to the facts, just noticing what is, without labeling it.

1. I am just noticing what is going on inside (sensations and thoughts). Notice any judgments you are making about yourself or others, then let them go.

2. I can describe what I notice in concrete, specific terms that are non-judgmental by:_____

3. Next, I am just noticing what is going on around me in my environment. I will let go of any judgments I am making about others.

4. I can describe what I notice in concrete, specific terms that are non-judgmental by:_____

5. "Observing and Describing" what is going on with me on the inside and the outside will assist me in being as effective as I can be:

_____

_____

Moment to Pause

D B T
I N
L I F E ™

This skill is about taking a "Moment to Pause" and check in with yourself both on the inside and the outside. By checking in with yourself on the inside and the outside, you can be responsive to what is going on and act in your own best interest.

You may feel like taking a "Moment to Pause" will take a lot of effort and really slow you down; however, once you learn this skill, you can do it in 1 to 2 seconds.

One way to take a "Moment to Pause" is to take a deep breath, notice thoughts, feelings, and impulses. Then take another deep breath to consider what is going on around you including interactions with others. Once you consider both of these things, you can decide what you want to do and say. You realize that you can act in a way that is most useful or effective.

Another way to accomplish the "Moment to Pause" is to count to 3 while noticing what is going on inside you. Next count to 4 or 6 while checking in on the outside. Last, decide what to say and what to do that will be most effective. Take a moment to practice this skill now.

Your assignment is take a "Moment to Pause" 3 times a day for the next week. Problem solve any difficulties. Consider how this skill is useful to you. Learn to do it more and more often. Using the "Moment to Pause" skill empowers you to be responsive instead of reactive in life.

Moment to Pause

Day	Record "Moment to Pause" experience 3x's daily Include any difficulties and helpfulness of the experience
Monday	
Tuesday	
Wednesday	
Thursday	
Friday	
Saturday	
Sunday	

D B T

I N

L I F E ™

ONE MIND

O = <u>O</u>ne Thing at a Time
N = Be in the <u>N</u>ow
E = Be Grounded in the <u>E</u>nvironment

M = Be <u>M</u>indfully Present in the Moment
I = <u>I</u>ncrease Your 5 Senses
N = Use my <u>N</u>on-Judgmental Skill
D = <u>D</u>escribe What is Going On in Words

Ways I can use this acronym to be skillful in my life:

_____

_____

_____

_____

_____

_____

_____

Participate

This skill is about participating fully in one activity at a time. It is about being active and involved in your life. Fully participating may mean that you have to challenge yourself to come out of your shell, face your fears, or combat your impulse to withdraw.

To effectively "Participate" in life, I will use my Observe, Describe, and Non-judgmental skills. By being present in the here and now on the inside and around me in a non-judgmental fashion I can invest myself in relationships, situations, and activities fully.

Relationships, situations and activities that I already "Participate" in fully:

_____

_____

Relationships, situations, and activities that I can "Participate" in more fully:

_____

_____

Ways I will do this:

_____

_____

_____

_____

Mindful Eating

"Mindful Eating" is about being fully present in the experience of eating. It is just eating. Noticing all 5 of your senses while eating. It is about fully appreciating the experience of eating. It is also about being non-judgmental with yourself before, during, and after eating.

1. Just eat, don't do anything else.
2. Notice what the food looks like.
3. Notice the scents or smells of the food.
4. Notice what it feels like in your hand or with a utensil.
5. Notice the weight, texture, and other sensations of the food in your mouth.
6. Notice salivation, taste, and any smells.
7. Chew each bite really well: 10, 15, or 20 chews.
8. Continue to eat the rest of your food by paying attention to all these experiences and sensations.
9. Notice any feelings of food in your stomach.
10. Notice feeling full and satiated.

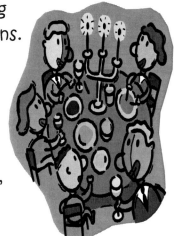

Practice this exercise with something small that you typically eat in handfuls: dried fruit, popcorn, nuts, chocolate, or chips.

Practice one mindful meal a week for 1 month.

Then practice 3 mindful meals a week for another month.

Ultimately, it may be useful to practice 1 mindful meal a day.

Mindful Eating

Things I noticed when I was "Mindfully Eating":

_____

_____

_____

Things that I was surprised by or didn't expect when eating mindfully:

_____

_____

_____

"Mindful Eating" will be useful to me by:

_____

_____

_____

Ways that I eat mindfully on regular basis:

_____

_____

_____

_____

One-Mindfully

This is the skill of focusing on one thing *in the moment.* While it might seem like multi-tasking is efficient, it is more effective to do one thing at a time, focusing on each thing by itself, than by moving onto the next thing. This can be done slowly or quickly depending on the task and your energy level.

Very few of us devote ourselves to living in the moment as life presents itself. Instead we do things automatically, without noticing what we are doing. We regularly do two or three things at once. Often times we get so caught up in our thoughts and feelings about the past or future that we get lost in them and become disconnected from what is happening right now in front of us. For example, you are in a session with your counselor. You are nodding your head in response but you're not really listening. Instead you are feeling self-conscious about how you look and are thinking about an argument you had the other day or an upcoming appointment. As a result you miss out on a moment of connection with a person who cares for you and instead have one more moment of living in the past with resentment and self criticism.

Practice living "One-Mindfully." The next time you are in a conversation with someone or in a treatment group, focus all your attention on the very moment you are in with that person or in the group. The next time you take a break, actually take a break. If you are worrying about things to come during your coffee break or moment of relaxation then you really never get a break. Much of the time when we are practicing being one-mindful we become distracted with other things such as thoughts, intense feelings, or urges. Let go of all distractions and bring yourself back to what you are doing. You may have to do this again, and again, and again.

D
B
T

I
N

L
I
F
E
™

One-Mindfully

While it might seem like multi-tasking is efficient, the research has shown that it isn't. It is more effective to do one thing at time, focusing on each thing by itself, than to move onto the next thing before you've finished with the first. This can be done slowly or quickly depending on the task and your energy level.

Do one thing at a time. When eating, eat. When driving, drive. When engaging in self-care, dedicate yourself to self-care. When at work, focus on the tasks at hand. When parenting, direct your energy and attention on each part of parenting in the moment. When using a skill, invest in doing just that skill in the moment.

Previous successes with doing one thing at a time:

_____

_____

Barriers and obstacles to doing one thing at a time:

_____

_____

Ideas to work around these barriers and obstacles:

_____

_____

Ways I am going to do one thing at time for the next week:

_____

_____

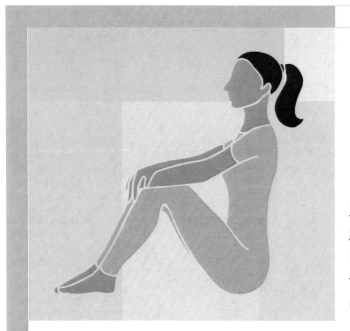

Body Scan

Let's take a few minutes to get grounded. That means understanding what is going on in the inside and around us in our environment.

First, go inside. Notice any pain, tension, or discomfort. Do not do anything about it, just make space for it. Second, notice any sensations of feeling at ease, relaxed, or comfortable. Do not try to create it, just make space for even the smallest amount. Third, notice any neutral sensations. The neutral sensations are the things you do not normally notice because they are neutral. Feel all the different sensations on the inside for a few moments.

Now turn your attention to the outside. Notice your feet on the ground. The feeling of being connected to the ground or with the furniture on which you are sitting. Notice your environment with your 5 senses: seeing, hearing, feeling, perhaps smell and taste. Become aware of any people around you. Take a few more moments to be present with yourself on the outside, then one more moment on the inside.

Practice this exercise at least once a day to get grounded in the here and now and act in your own best interest.

D
B
T

I N

L
I
F
E
™

Body Scan and Square Breathing

Barriers and obstacles to using these skills:

_____

_____

_____

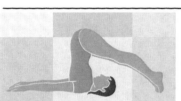

Ways to overcome these barriers and obstacles:

_____

_____

_____

Strategies for practicing these skills on a regular basis.

_____

_____

_____

Turtling

Turtles use a variety of strategies to take care of themselves.
They withdraw inside themselves and re-emerge cautiously
They protect themselves through snapping and biting
They are adaptive by living in water and on land
Let things roll off their hard outer shell
Move slowly and intentionally
Persistently self-righting

When turtles are self-righting, they will use any support they can find to flip themselves over when life has turned them upside down.

Ways I will use a variety of "Turtling" strategies to take care of myself and be effective in my life:

_____

_____

_____

_____

_____

Turtling

Draw yourself as a turtle who is about to take care of him/herself using a variety of "Turtling" strategies.

Wise Mind

This skill is about balancing thinking and feeling. DBT believes that we are more effective in our lives when we have both thinking and feeling in our experience.

An example of this is Captain Kirk from the original Star Trek series. Captain Kirk is typically in a state of "Wise Mind." Spock, the Vulcan, represents logic and thinking (our rational mind). McCoy, the doctor, represents feelings and passion (our emotional mind). Kirk takes information from both the logical and feeling perspective to act in his and others' best interest.

Another example is from Harry Potter. Hermione is very thoughtful and Ron is emotional. Harry uses his best friends to make sense of what is happening and decide how he should respond.

Successes with being in "Wise Mind," even when I didn't know it:

_____

_____

Strategies for increasing thinking when out of balance with too much emotion or feelings:

_____

_____

Strategies for increasing positive emotions when out of balance with too much thinking:

_____

_____

Wise Mind

Benefits of being almost entirely in emotional mind:

_____

_____

Costs of being almost entirely in emotional mind:

_____

_____

Benefits of being almost entirely in rational mind:

_____

_____

Costs of being almost entirely in rational mind:

_____

_____

Benefits of being in "Wise Mind":

_____

_____

Costs of being in "Wise Mind":

_____

_____

Effectively   Effectively

This skill is about being as effective as possible. It is focusing on what is most useful. It is about keeping your eye on the ball and not sweating the little stuff. It is about balancing short-term and long-term goals as well as what is important now. It's doing what works instead of doing what we *feel* like doing and regretting it later.

What is important to me:

_____

Less effective strategies that I might use to accomplish this/these:

_____

_____

What are some more "Effective" strategies that I can use instead:

_____

_____

How will I use more "Effective" strategies instead of less effective strategies in my life:

_____

_____

Be Mindful

"Be Mindful" is about being aware of and paying attention to what is going on with you and in your life. You can be mindful of using a skill, engaging in self-care, having effective interactions, or other things.

It would be useful for me to "Be Mindful" of:

1. _____

2. _____

3. _____

Remember to do these one thing at time.

Ways that I can "Be Mindful" of these:

_____

_____

_____

Non-Judgmental

D
B
T

I
N

L
I
F
E
™

Being "Non-Judgmental" is about not assigning a value to yourself or others such as being good, bad, terrible, or unlovable. Making judgments or assigning value to yourself or others causes unnecessary distress and discomfort.

Behavior can be judged as good or bad, right or wrong, useful or useless, but it is unnecessary and ineffective to judge the person engaging in the behavior. Behavior can generate natural and logical consequences that are both good and bad. Instead of making judgments, describe what is going on, how you feel about it, and how you want to respond to it, without assigning value to yourself or others. Examples:

"I am very unhappy that this happened to me," instead of "I am a complete idiot because this happened to me."

"That person disrespected me and that is not OK with me," instead of "That person is a complete jerk."

Positive judgments are just as problematic as negative judgments. If you judge positively, you are at risk of also making negative judgments. The best advice is to skip the judgment, describe what is going on and identify your feelings. Once you have done this you can be as effective as possible in the relationship or situation.

Mindfulness Skills

Non-Judgmental

Previous successes in being "Non-Judgmental" with myself:

_____

_____

Barriers and obstacles to being "Non-Judgmental" with myself:

_____

_____

Ideas to work around these barriers and obstacles:

_____

_____

Previous successes being "Non-Judgmental" with others:

_____

_____

Barriers and obstacles to being "Non-Judgmental" with others:

_____

_____

Ideas to work around these barriers and obstacles:

_____

_____

Non-Judgmental

Being "Non-Judgmental" is about not assigning a value to yourself or others. Using judgments can be isolating and problematic. The judgments people might make of themselves may confirm their beliefs that they are failures, terrible, or unlovable. This can make engaging in problematic, harmful behaviors justified.

Instead of putting a value on yourself or others, you can describe what is going on. Remember descriptions can include opinions about whether or not you like something or disagree with it. Being "Non-Judgmental" doesn't mean that everything is pleasant and there are no problems. Non-judgmental just means that you don't have to put a label on yourself or others as being good or bad.

Let's try an exercise of identifying judgments and replacing them with a description. Below are some examples.

Judgment: "I am a terrible parent."
Description: "I don't have all the answers about how to parent."

Judgment: "I am a complete failure, I deserve to be unhappy."
Descriptions: "Sometimes I make mistakes."

Judgment: "My boss is a complete idiot."
Description: "My boss doesn't understand how hard I am working."

Judgment: "My family is the worst ever."

Description: "My family does things that hurt me and I'm mad about it."

Non-Judgmental

D
B
T

I
N

L
I
F
E
™

About me:

A judgment that I make about myself:

_____

A replacement description:

_____

A judgment that I make about myself:

_____

A replacement description:

_____

About others:

A judgment that I make about others:

_____

A replacement description:

_____

A judgment that I make about others:

_____

_____

A replacement description:

_____

_____

Mindfulness Skills Word Search

```
N  R  K  D  E  S  C  R  I  B  E  J  X  Y  C  P  M
E  F  F  E  C  T  I  V  E  L  Y  R  Y  D  B  K  I
D  M  G  L  K  L  N  M  R  L  P  H  Z  J  B  Y  N
K  S  Q  U  A  R  E  B  R  E  A  T  H  I  N  G  D
N  N  O  N  -  J  U  D  G  M  E  N  T  A  L  W  F
R  M  N  M  K  N  H  C  C  T  T  J  H  T  R  Z  U
N  N  E  P  P  X  L  M  B  R  U  Q  N  E  W  L  L
C  Y  M  J  P  A  W  R  J  O  D  R  V  B  U  T  E
P  P  I  F  R  R  R  P  K  N  D  R  T  F  N  L  A
K  W  N  C  K  W  M  T  I  K  E  Y  D  L  H  B  T
N  I  D  H  N  N  C  M  I  S  C  N  S  X  I  V  I
Z  S  F  K  Q  C  E  P  B  C  I  M  N  C  Z  N  N
P  E  U  M  P  N  V  O  F  M  I  M  N  C  A  C  G
H  M  L  L  O  M  D  N  E  J  X  P  W  V  Y  N  R
Q  I  L  K  F  C  G  B  D  M  K  M  A  B  Z  T  H
F  N  Y  N  F  Z  H  G  T  L  F  L  H  T  M  R  B
T  D  M  O  M  E  N  T  T  O  P  A  U  S  E  F  J
```

www.WordSearchMaker.com

Be Mindful	Observe
Body Scan	ONE MIND
Describe	One Mindfully
Effectively	Participate
Mindful Eating	Square Breathing
Moment to Pause	Turtling
Non-Judgmental	Wise Mind

Mindfulness Skills Word Search Answers

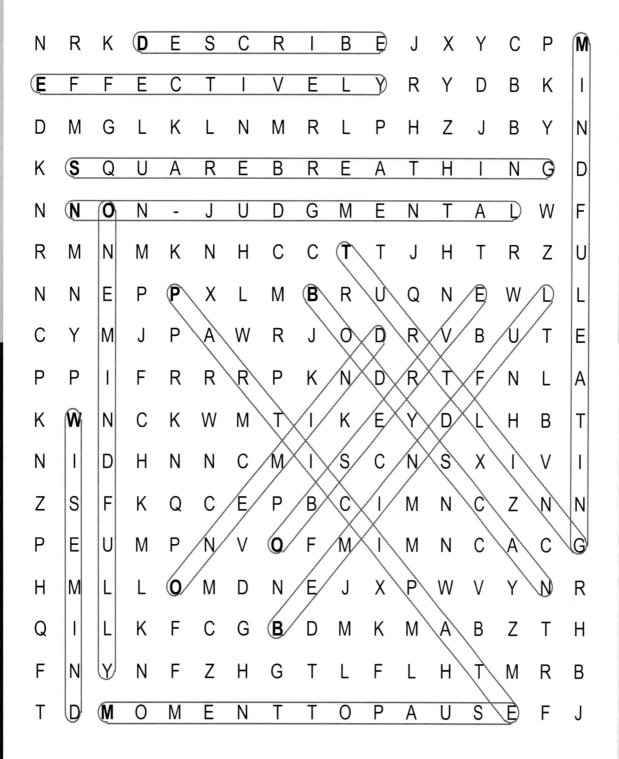

D
B
T

I
N

L
I
F
E
™

Mindfulness Skills Crossword Puzzle

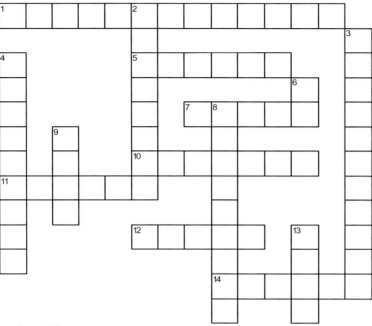

www.CrosswordWeaver.com

ACROSS

1 I am learning to not assign a value to myself and others by being _____.

5 The I in ONE MIND stands for?

7 By using my Moment to _____ skill I can check in with myself to be responsive rather reactive in my life.

10 Wise Mind is about _____ thoughts and feelings.

11 I can be skill like a _____ by withdrawing into myself and cautiously re-emerge when it safe.

12 One mindfully is about doing one _____ at a time.

14 _____ Breathing is when I take a take a long slow breath while counting to 4.

DOWN

2 Observe and _____ help me be grounded within myself and in environment.

3 I can fully _____ in my life.

4 One of my biggest goals for using my DBT skills is to be as _____ as possible in my life.

6 _____ Mindful is about being aware of self care and other important activities I engage in.

8 Mindfulness increases my _____ of my thoughts, feelings, behaviors and relationships.

9 Through Mindfulness and DBT I am learning to let go of less effective strategies for _____ effective ones.

13 I can practice Mindfulness though Body _____.O

Mindfulness Skills Crossword Puzzle Answers

```
N O N J U D G M E N T A L
            E                 P
E           S E N S E S       A
F           C             B   R
F           R     P A U S E   T
E     M     I     W           I
C     O     B A L A N C E     C
T U R T L E       R           I
I     E           E           P
V           T H I N G     S   A
E                 E       C   T
                  S Q U A R E
                  S       N
```

Practicing Mindfulness

Mindfulness is about voluntarily, purposefully, and intentionally being present in today. It is a form of awareness of the moment. This is done in a non-judgmental fashion. When focusing on the past or the future, it is done intentionally and for no longer than is effective. Mindfulness is training your mind to pay attention to what you choose, instead of your mind controlling you.

Things that I enjoy the most about Mindfulness:

_____

_____

Difficulties I have had practicing mindfulness daily:

_____

_____

Ways to problem solve and overcome these difficulties:

_____

_____

Some of my successes with mindfulness are:

_____

_____

Ways I can have more successes:

_____

_____

D
B
T

I
N

L
I
F
E
™

My Mindfulness

My favorite Mindfulness skills are:

_____

_____

_____

_____

Ways that I use these skills are:

_____

_____

_____

_____

CHAPTER 5

Distress Tolerance Worksheets

Distress Tolerance Skills

Distress tolerance is about frustration tolerance. Having frustration tolerance is an essential life skill for everyone. Frustration tolerance means being able to hold frustration and stress without engaging in negative, problematic, or destructive behavior. Some frustrations can be tolerated while other frustrations can be modulated. Frustration tolerance is accomplished by balancing active strategies and willingness when you are dealing with problems, stress, drama, or crises.

Active strategies include focusing on problem solving. Finding effective ways to cope and manage the problems, stress, drama, or crises. Skills that are useful to actively solving problems and difficulties are:

- Exploring Pros and Cons
- Crisis Survival Network
- Keeping It In Perspective
- Half Smile
- OBJECTIVES
- SPECIFIC PATHS

Willingness teaches you that sometimes you get what you want, sometimes others get it their way, and whenever possible both you and others getting what they want is optimal. Willingness is also about being able to say "No," being disappointed, or not getting what you want. Using willingness is very helpful when active strategies don't work. Examples of skills that facilitate this are:

- Self-Soothe
- Self-Soothe Kit
- Observe Breathing
- ACCEPTS
- IMPROVE
- Willingness
- Radical Acceptance

Distress Tolerance Skills

Pros & Cons

Pros of Having Drama & Stress	Cons of Not Having Drama & Stress
Cons of Having Drama & Stress	Pros of Not Having Drama & Stress

Distress Tolerance Skills

Observe Breathing

This exercise is designed to help you deal with crises, stressful situations, and/or difficulties. When you find yourself in one of these situations, you can cope with it by getting grounded in your breathing. This will orient you to the present moment, serve as a distraction from the stress and introduce a calming effect. The calming effect is achieved by providing more oxygen to the mind and body thus reducing anxiety and distressing bodily sensations. Here are some ways you can observe your breathing.

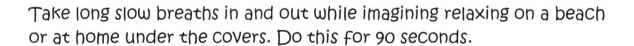

Inhale while counting to 5 slowly.
Let the breath out while counting to 5 slowly.
Repeat 5 times.

Take a deep breath while taking one long stride.
Let out the breath while taking one long stride.
Repeat 3 times.

Take long slow breaths in and out while imagining relaxing on a beach or at home under the covers. Do this for 90 seconds.

For every distressing thought or painful sensation complete a full deep breath in and out.

First practice this skill at times when you are not under a great deal of stress. This way you will be prepared next time a crisis or stressful situation occurs.

Distress Tolerance Skills

Willingness

"Willingness" is about being open and accepting doing what is needed (even if it means stepping outside your comfort zone). It also means tolerating when you don't get your way or things don't happen the way you think they "should." It is about going with the flow and not fighting reality.

By comparison, willfulness is about struggling and fighting against yourself, others, and the world around you; demanding that things "go *your* way." Let's explore how both of these work in your life.

I am being willful when: _____

_____

Some of the benefits of being willful: _____

_____

Some of the costs of being willful:_____

_____

Ways willing behavior looks different : _____

_____

I am being willing when: _____

_____

Some benefits of being willing are: _____

_____

I can bring more "Willingness" into my life by: _____

Distress Tolerance Skills

Self-Soothe

This skill is about self-soothing when you are having a bad day or dealing with a lot of stress. Self-soothing provides comfort and reassurance. It can help you stay grounded in your body and in the present moment. It can serve as a distraction from the difficulties you are dealing with.

The "Self-Soothe" skill is about using all 5 of your senses to "Self-Soothe": Seeing, hearing, smelling, touching, & tasting.

Ideas for self-soothing through sight:
Pictures, Art, Stargazing, etc.

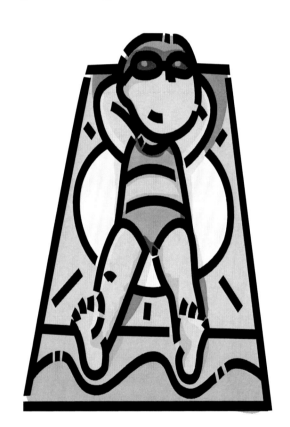

Ideas for self-soothing through sound:
Music, Nature Sounds, etc.

Ideas for self-soothing through smells:
Fragrance, Food Aromas, etc.

Ideas for self-soothing through touch:
Fabric, Rocks, Hands, Pets, etc.

Ideas for self-soothing through taste:
Sweet, Sour, Chewy foods, etc.

The ways in which you choose to "Self-Soothe" will need to be effective and not cause additional problems for you. For example, if you tend to overeat, then you might not want to "Self-Soothe" with food.

Distress Tolerance Skills

Self-Soothe

I can "Self-Soothe" with vision by:

_____

_____

I can "Self-Soothe" with sound by:

_____

_____

I can "Self-Soothe" with smells by:

_____

_____

I can "Self-Soothe" with touch by:

_____

_____

I can "Self-Soothe" with taste by:

_____

_____

Distress Tolerance Skills

OBJECTIVES

You can effectively deal with difficult experiences by using this acronym. It helps to practice using the acronym before you really need it.

<u>O</u>ne thing at a time
<u>B</u>e effective
avoid <u>J</u>udgments
cope with <u>E</u>motions
consider <u>C</u>onsequences
take <u>T</u>ime
use <u>I</u>ntrospection
act consistently with <u>V</u>alues
focus on desired <u>E</u>ndings
balance <u>S</u>hort-term and long-term goals

Distress Tolerance Skills

OBJECTIVES

I can do <u>O</u>ne thing at a time by:

_____

_____

I can <u>B</u>e effective and avoid <u>J</u>udgments by:

_____

_____

I can cope with <u>E</u>motions and consider <u>C</u>onsequences by:

_____

_____

I can take <u>T</u>ime, use <u>I</u>ntrospection, and act consistently with <u>V</u>alues by:

_____

_____

I can focus on desired <u>E</u>ndings by:

_____

_____

I can balance <u>S</u>hort-term and long-term goals by:

_____

_____

D.B.T. in Life™

Distress Tolerance Skills

SPECIFIC PATHS

This acronym will help you stay on the path to building the life you want for yourself.

what is my **S**upreme Concern?
Practice my skills
focus my **E**nergy and **C**oncentration
I can be effective
have **F**aith
figure out what is **I**mportant
have **C**ourage and **P**atience
pay **A**ttention
complete **T**asks
be **H**umble and have **S**ensitivity

D.B.T. in Life™

Distress Tolerance Skills

SPECIFIC PATHS

My Supreme concern or what is most important to me is:

_____

I can Practice my skills by:

_____

I can focus my Energy and Concentration by:

_____

I can be effective by:

_____

I can have Faith by:

_____

I can figure out what is Important by:

_____

I can have Courage and Patience by:

_____

I can pay Attention to the environment and myself by:

_____

I can complete Tasks by:

_____

I can be Humble and have Sensitivity by:

_____

Distress Tolerance Skills

ACCEPTS

This acronym is designed to distract you from difficulties or stress. Fully participate in each letter as a way to get a break from what you find hard to deal with in the moment. Once you have had a break and feel grounded return to the difficulty to solve or manage it more effectively.

A = <u>A</u>ctivities
C = <u>C</u>ontributions
C = <u>C</u>hoices
E = <u>E</u>motions
P = <u>P</u>ushing <u>A</u>way
T = <u>T</u>houghts
S = <u>S</u>ensations

<u>A</u>ctivities: Reading, exercising, watching TV, or something fun, etc.

<u>C</u>ontributions: Do something for yourself, others, or your surroundings.

<u>C</u>hoices: Choose your thoughts, feelings, and behaviors wisely.

<u>E</u>motions: Find ways to increase your positive emotions.

<u>P</u>ushing <u>A</u>way: Emotionally or physically push away the crisis or stress.

<u>T</u>houghts: Shift your thinking towards something enjoyable.

<u>S</u>ensations: Get grounded in what you are feeling in your body.

ACCEPTS

<u>A</u>ctivities I can distract myself with:

_____

_____

I can distract myself with <u>C</u>ontributions of doing something for others, the environment, or myself by:

_____

_____

<u>C</u>hoices I can distract myself with:

_____

_____

Positive <u>E</u>motions I can distract myself with:

_____

_____

I can <u>P</u>ush <u>A</u>way stress by:

_____

_____

<u>T</u>houghts I can distract myself with:

_____

_____

<u>S</u>ensations I can distract myself with:

_____

D.B.T. in Life™

Distress Tolerance Skills

IMPROVE

I = **I**magery
M = **M**eaning
P = **P**rayer
R = **R**elaxation
O = **O**ne-Mindfully
V = **V**acation
E = **E**ncouragement

This acronym is designed to provide relief when you are having a bad day or something goes wrong.

Imagery: Use visualization and imagery to take a break.

Meaning: Identify meaning and purpose in your life.

Prayer: Use formally or informally to ask for help or feel connected.

Relaxation: Remember to breathe. Do things that are relaxing and enjoyable.

One-Mindfully: Focus on just one thing at a time.

Vacation: Take time for yourself. It can be a few minutes or much longer.

Encouragement: Positive self-talk and support from others can be useful.

Distress Tolerance Skills
IMPROVE

Imagery will help me by:

_____

_____

I can identify Meaning in my life by:

_____

_____

I can use Prayer or connection with something by:

_____

_____

I use Relaxation when:

_____

_____

One-Mindfully helps me by:

_____

_____

I can take short or long Vacations to manage stress by:

_____

_____

I can accept Encouragement from myself and others by:

_____

Distress Tolerance Skills

Self-Soothe 1ˢᵗ Aid Kit

You can think of this skill as "1ˢᵗ Aid Kit" or "tool kit." Use this skill to make a kit that is self-soothing. This can be a box of stuff, an envelope that can be kept in a wallet or purse, or files on an mp3 player or laptop. Things that you may want to put in the kit are pictures of friends, family members, pets, or special places; a favorite song or book; craft supplies, sports equipment, etc. The things that you have in your kit should only be helpful, not hurtful in any way. Once you have created your kit, you can use it when you are feeling stress, something goes wrong, or you have any impulse to act in problematic ways.

Items for my "Self-Soothe 1st Aid" or "Self-Soothe Tool Kit" are:

_____

_____

_____

_____

_____

_____

Ways I will use my "Self-Soothe 1st Aid" or "Self-Soothe Tool Kit" are:

_____

_____

_____

Distress Tolerance Skills

Turning The Mind

You are in the driver's seat with your thinking, feeling, impulses, and behaviors. You can decide which road you are driving on. If your current road isn't effective for you then take the left-hand exit, right-hand exit, make a U-turn, or pull over and stop for awhile. These are all opportunities for you to get on a different road of thinking, feeling, or behaving. All of these maneuvers are encouraged, but only if they are more effective than the road you are currently on.

If I stay on my current road of thinking, feeling, impulse, or behavior it will likely lead me where?

_____

How will turning to the right or left, turning around completely, or pulling over to park for awhile help me get to where I want to go with a change in my thinking, feeling, impulses, and behavior?

_____

_____

Taking a right turn at what exit puts me on a road toward effective thoughts, feelings, impulses, and behaviors:

_____

_____

Taking a left turn at what exit puts me on a road of these effective thoughts, feelings, impulses, and behaviors:

_____

_____

By pulling over to park, I can think, feel, and behave these ways:

_____

_____

D.B.T. in Life™

Distress Tolerance Skills

Turning The Mind

Draw the road that you take when you are being ineffective, having problems, or damaging relationships. Label what thoughts, feelings, and behaviors you are engaging in along this road.

D.B.T. in Life™

Distress Tolerance Skills

Turning The Mind

Now draw the road that you can take to be more effective. Label what thoughts, feelings, and behaviors you are engaging in along this road.

Distress Tolerance Skills

Crisis Survival Network

Most people in life can benefit from having a "Crisis Survival Network" (CSN). This is a list of people who support you in the middle of a crisis or a problem. Compile a list of people and their contact information so that you can connect with them as needed. One suggestion is to have a variety of people on your list such as family, friends, coworkers, peer counselors, sponsors, mentors, acquaintances, teachers, and others. Another suggestion is to use the list flexibly. Don't just get in touch with the same person over and over again. Use everyone on the list a little bit and in different ways. A third suggestion is to be reciprocal when you can. Support the people on your CSN when possible.

My CSN includes these people and their contact info:

_____

_____

_____

_____

_____

_____

_____

I will use my CSN when:

_____

_____

_____

Distress Tolerance Skills

Crisis Survival Network

When I am having a bad day, having a difficult time, or feel an urge to act problematically:

Support meetings I can attend:

_____

_____

Support I can access on the Internet:

_____

_____

Supportive people I can call or visit:

_____

_____

Activities I can do:

_____

_____

Skills I can use:

_____

_____

_____

D.B.T. in Life™

Distress Tolerance Skills

Half Smile

Even in the middle of a difficult situation or stress, you can probably find something to be a little bit happy about or something that is enjoyable. Like many of the DBT skills, this one is about having balance. When things are hard, think of things that are easy. When you don't get what you want remember a time when you did. When you are in pain imagine also being relaxed.

This skill is about finding at least one little thing to have a small and genuine smile about. It could be something in the past, something happening right now, or even something in the future. You hold this small "Half Smile" with the stress and difficulty you are currently experiencing.

By having a small genuine "Half Smile" on your face, you are less tense in your face, neck, and shoulders. You may also find that people treat you differently and that you interact with others differently when you have a "Half Smile" on your face.

Things that I can have a genuine "Half Smile" about:

_____

_____

_____

_____

_____

_____

_____

Distress Tolerance Skills

Half Smile

Barriers and obstacles to using the "Half Smile" skill effectively:

_____

_____

_____

_____

_____

Strategies to overcome the barriers and obstacles:

_____

_____

_____

_____

_____

Ways I will use "Half Smile" effectively on a regular basis:

_____

_____

_____

_____

Distress Tolerance Skills

Radical Acceptance

This skill is about identifying what you have control over, what you don't have control over, and knowing the difference between these two. There are many things in life that are out of your control, including people and the environment. What you do have control over is yourself. You can control your thinking, feelings, impulses, and behaviors.

"Radical Acceptance" is about being skillful by letting go of things you can't control in order to focus your energy on what you can control: Yourself.

"Radical Acceptance" is empowering and life enhancing. It is not approval or resignation. It doesn't mean that you have to like what is happening. It is accepting that reality is what it is. Then you can focus on being who you need to be and acting how you need to act to be as effective as possible.

Strategies I will use to let go of things I can't control:

_____

_____

_____

_____

Strategies to stay in control of my thinking, feeling, impulses, and behavior:

_____

_____

_____

_____

Distress Tolerance Skills

Radical Acceptance

Barriers and obstacles to using "Radical Acceptance" effectively:

_____

_____

_____

Strategies to overcome the barriers and obstacles:

_____

_____

_____

_____

Ways I will use "Radical Acceptance" effectively on a regular basis:

_____

_____

_____

_____

D.B.T. in Life™

Distress Tolerance Skills

Keeping It In Perspective

This skill is about remembering life is all a matter of perspective.

What you are going through right now might not have been as bad as what you have dealt with in the past. If this is the case, think about how your previous experiences can help you deal with this situation.

Perhaps this is the worst it has ever been. If that is the case, then you can use the smaller difficulties that you have survived and overcome as practice for this current situation. It is almost like this is the marathon of difficulties and everything you have been through up to now has been training for this situation.

I can use my previous experience and skills to be effective now by:

_____

_____

_____

Ways I can get additional help if needed:

_____

_____

_____

D.B.T. in Life™

Distress Tolerance Skills

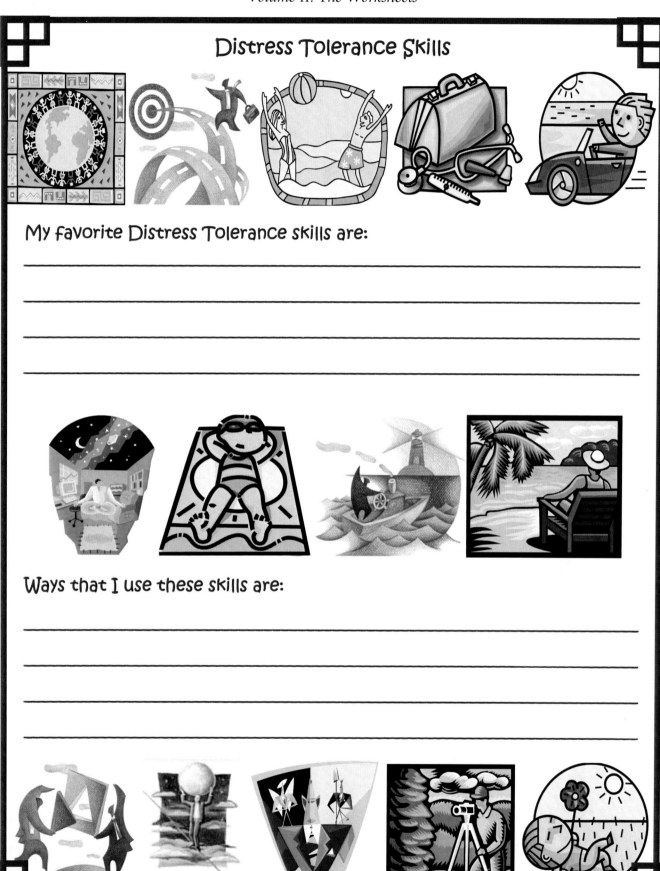

My favorite Distress Tolerance skills are:

_____

_____

_____

_____

Ways that I use these skills are:

_____

_____

_____

_____

D.B.T. in Life™

Distress Tolerance Skills Word Search

```
C  R  I  S  I  S  S  U  R  V  I  V  A  L  N  E  T  W  O  R  K
O  B  S  E  R  V  E  B  R  E  A  T  H  I  N  G  P  K  M  L  D
G  R  X  S  E  L  F  S  O  O  T  H  E  K  I  T  Y  T  X  N  K
Z  A  V  J  T  L  Y  H  M  C  J  N  Y  A  P  T  T  W  I  K  E
Q  D  T  H  A  L  F  S  M  I  L  E  Y  K  C  Y  V  M  V  C  E
Y  I  K  G  Z  T  Y  N  V  Z  N  T  R  R  R  C  E  R  V  L  P
G  C  N  S  E  L  F  S  O  O  T  H  E  M  R  H  E  Z  H  S  I
K  A  L  T  H  C  D  M  J  M  N  D  Q  R  T  T  C  P  H  G  T
R  L  C  C  P  B  G  L  M  K  N  T  Y  G  K  C  R  T  T  H  I
M  A  V  P  M  Z  T  H  N  M  R  Z  N  V  P  Y  A  M  H  S  N
Y  C  F  O  W  M  Z  M  Q  T  B  I  H  S  B  P  Q  M  D  W  P
M  C  D  B  G  I  R  R  T  D  N  D  N  L  C  Y  G  T  Z  G  E
T  E  F  J  R  V  L  P  V  R  J  O  D  I  I  M  C  L  Y  T  R
K  P  B  E  R  D  L  L  U  C  C  K  F  K  M  G  N  Z  Y  Y  S
Z  T  N  C  D  N  F  T  I  D  G  I  L  T  P  Z  M  T  T  K  P
F  A  T  T  F  T  T  K  N  N  C  T  N  K  R  Q  L  P  R  Q  E
Q  N  D  I  T  Z  G  A  K  E  G  K  K  K  O  L  C  V  Q  V  C
X  C  G  V  M  Q  S  T  P  J  X  N  N  D  V  Z  K  Y  M  Q  T
V  E  N  E  G  O  T  S  Q  N  M  F  E  N  E  K  G  F  Y  K  I
B  R  L  S  R  T  R  K  M  T  R  N  M  S  C  N  N  C  K  J  V
Z  W  N  P  R  N  N  L  T  W  Q  N  T  S  R  D  J  D  R  E
```

ACCEPTS	Pros and Cons
Crisis Survival Network	Radical Acceptance
Half Smile	Self Soothe
IMPROVE	Self Soothe Kit
Keep It In Perspective	SPECIFIC PATHS
OBJECTIVES	Turning the Mind
Observe Breathing	Willingness

D.B.T. in Life™

Distress Tolerance Skills Word Search Answers

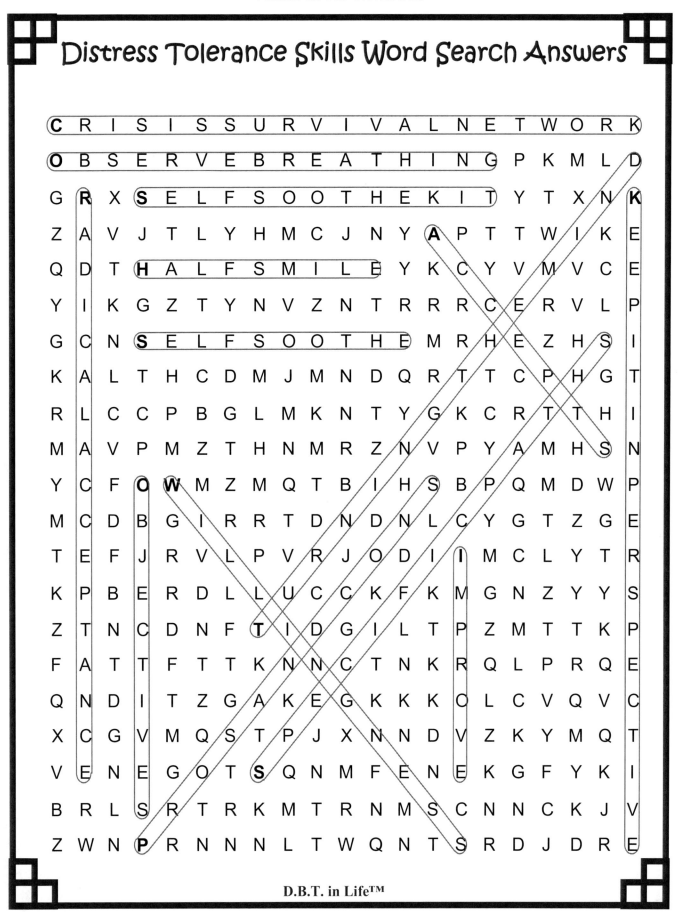

Distress Tolerance Skills Crossword Puzzle

ACROSS

1 I can find something to have a _____ - Smile about even when I am having a bad day.

6 Keeping It In _____ skill helps me see that I have been training to deal with these difficulties or a big crisis.

8 I can _____ Breathing to manage stress.

10 _____ and Cons explores the positives and negatives of staying the same or changing.

11 The V in IMPROVE stands for _____.

12 My Crisis _____ Network supports me when I am having difficulties.

13 When I use the Turning the _____ skill I can change the road my thoughts, feelings, and behaviors are on to the road that is more effective for me.

14 The J in OBJECTIVES reminds me to be Non-_____.

DOWN

2 The A in ACCEPTS means that I can distract myself by engaging in _____.

3 Using my Distress Tolerance skills helps me tolerate _____.

4 I can create a Self-Soothe _____ to help feel better when I am having a crisis or a lot of problems.

5 I use all 5 of my _____ to Self-Soothe when I am stressed out.

7 _____ is about getting it my way sometimes and tolerating when I don't.

9 _____ Acceptance teaches me to focus my energy on what I can change: my thoughts, feelings, and actions.

10 The P in SPECIFIC reminds that me that I can _____ my skills on a daily basis.

D.B.T. in Life™

140

Distress Tolerance Skills Crossword Answers

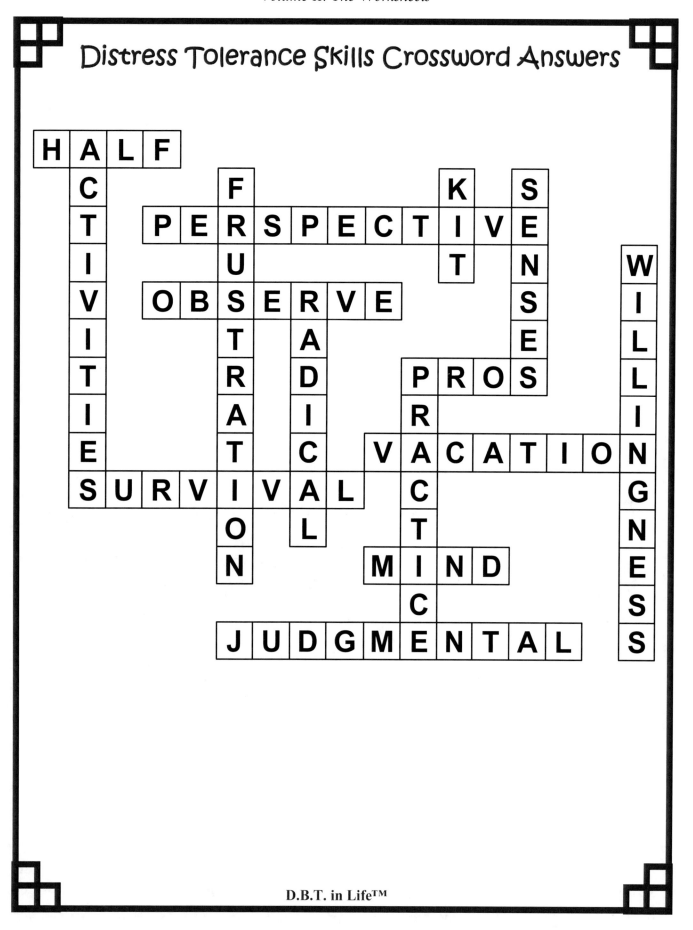

Distress Tolerance Skills

CHAPTER 6

Emotional Regulation Worksheets

D
B
T

I
N

L
I
F
E
™

Emotional regulation helps you learn about your emotions, achieve a deeper understanding of their emotional life, and develop more resiliency when dealing with your emotions. Emotions are part of life. You might believe that you shouldn't have any emotions, or that your should only have positive emotions. When you have unpleasant or painful emotions such anger, sadness, or loneliness, you can accept these emotions without engaging in problematic, destructive behavior.

Through emotional regulation you will learn impulse control and to delay gratification. As part of this process you will explore how you can feel a strong impulse or strong emotion without acting on it. You can learn to tolerate the impulses or emotions, which would be the "Riding the Wave" skill. By riding the wave, you can harness the energy, impulse, or emotion; stay mindfully present with it; and be patient until it shifts into the next impulse or emotion in the same way the tides shift. When dealing with difficult or painful emotions you can choose to use a DBT skill to deal with them. The skills that facilitate emotional regulation and impulse control are:

- ABC
- CARES
- TRUST
- MEDDSS
- BEHAVIOR
- EMOTIONS
- Lemonade
- Love Dandelions
- Feeling not Acting
- Opposite to Emotions
- Exploring My Emotions
- Build Positive Emotions
- Getting to Know My Emotions

Feeling Not Acting

This skill is about moving away from being reactive and moving toward being more responsive. It is about learning that an impulse and an action are two different things. It may seem like it happens all at once, but it is actually two steps. First you experience an impulse. The second step is the action or behavior you engage in. This skill is about slowing down the process and engaging more deliberate actions.

By using the "Moment to Pause" skill, you can take a deep breath while checking in with yourself to identify and feel your impulse(s), whatever the impulse(s) may be.

Next, you can decide what you want to do with the impulse(s).

1. You can "Ride the Wave" of the impulse(s) to let it runs its course without acting on it.

2. You can use another skill, such as "Crisis Survival Network" or "Self Soothe 1st Aid Kit, to effectively deal with the impulse(s).

3. You can act on the impulse in less problematic ways.

D
B
T

I
N

L
I
F
E
™

ABC

A = Accumulate Positives
B = Build Mastery
C = Cope Ahead

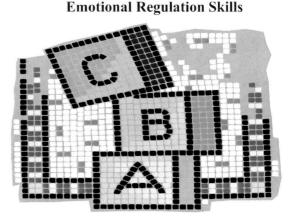

D
B
T

I
N

L
I
F
E
™

Accumulate Positives: This letter of the skill is about having a bank account of positive experiences that you have been saving up to make a withdrawal from when you need to balance out an upsetting situation. One example of accumulate positives would be getting a free airline ticket for getting bumped from your flight. The next time you have difficulty flying you can remember that you got a free ticket. Another example would be getting feedback that you did really well on a project or school assignment. You can use this to balance out the next time you don't do something well.

Build Mastery: This component of the skill is about thinking about or doing something that you are good at. By thinking or doing something that you are good at, you are facilitating healthy self-esteem. This boosts your confidence to get through times that are difficult. A couple of examples of Build Mastery would be realizing that you are very creative or that you are committed to being the best parent you can be. Realizing that there are things that you are good at helps to balance out negative feedback or a problematic situation.

Cope Ahead: Develop plans to deal with expected and unexpected difficulties. Here are three examples of cope ahead: Having a roadside assistance program so that you can get your car towed if it breaks down. Having overdraft protection on your checking account in case you are overdrawn. Backing up computer files in case your computer crashes.

Emotional Regulation Skills

ABC

A = **A**ccumulate Positives
B = **B**uild Mastery
C = **C**ope Ahead

Ways I can **A**ccumulate positives:

_____

_____

_____

_____

Ways I can **B**uild mastery:

_____

_____

_____

_____

Ways I can **C**ope ahead:

_____

_____

_____

_____

Getting to Know My Emotions

This skill is about getting to know your emotions. Sometimes people don't know very much about their emotions and they are unable to determine how they feel. Other times, people feel like they can only have a couple of emotions but not all of them. Emotions and feelings aren't good or bad, they just are what they are. The behavior people engage in as an expression of their emotions may be good or bad. This skill is about helping you know your emotions so that you can deal with them effectively and avoid engaging in problematic behaviors.

D B T

I N

L I F E™

1. Determine what is happening in the environment. Figure out what happened in your surroundings just prior to your current emotional state.

2. Identify and describe your emotions and feelings in concrete language that is non-judgmental.

3. Be grounded in your body. Notice how you experience your emotions and feelings physically.

4. Pay attention to your thoughts. Become aware of what thoughts you have when experiencing your emotions and feelings.

5. Next, evaluate your behavior. Figure out how emotions and feelings influence behavior. Evaluate if your behavior is as effective as it could be. If not, figure out other behavior that would be more effective. Implement any DBT skills here that could be useful.

6. Think about the potential aftermath. If you feel, think, and behave in a particular way, consider what the aftermath might be. If it is a problematic aftermath, determine alternative feelings, thoughts, and behaviors that would reduce or eliminate negative outcomes.

Emotional Regulation Skills

Love Dandelions

This is a metaphor about how the more you try to control something the more it may control you. In gardening the plants that are the most resilient are the weeds; in the lawn it's the dandelions that are the most resilient. You could spend a lot of time and energy trying to rid the lawn of the dandelions, but you will probably still have dandelions. Obsessing about getting rid of all dandelions can significantly lower your quality of life.

Individuals have dandelions in their lives. Dandelions are traits, habits, or behaviors that are problematic, but can't be completely eliminated. An example of a personal dandelion is addiction. Someone with an addiction can get into recovery; however, they have to work on a daily basis to not return to their addictive lifestyle. Other dandelions could be self-harm behavior, difficulties with food, being reactive, wanting to win, perfectionism, among others. It is essential to identify your dandelions to develop effective strategies to manage the dandelions.

Some of my dandelions are:

_____

_____

_____

Strategies to effectively cope with my dandelions are:

_____

_____

_____

D
B
T

I
N

L
I
F
E
™

Lemonade

This skill requires you to make "Lemonade" out of lemons. You can take a weakness in your life and turn it into a strength which empowers you to be more effective in your life.

An example of a lemon would be being in a lot of pain. Making that into "Lemonade" would be using the ability to tolerate pain to work hard in therapy.

Another example of a lemon would be being mistreated or traumatized. Making that into "Lemonade" would be surviving and then using your success with surviving to help others.

One more example would be a lemon of criminal behavior. Making that into "Lemonade" would be turning that into success in business.

Some movies containing examples of "Lemonade" are:
- Catch Me if You Can
- Forrest Gump
- North Country
- Shrek
- Beautiful Mind
- Pursuit of Happyness
- Happy Feet
- Freedom Writers
- Beautiful Mind
- Norma Rae
- Ray
- Other Examples?

D
B
T

I
N

L
I
F
E
™

Emotional Regulation Skills

Lemonade

Turning your weaknesses into strengths is the skill of turning lemons into "Lemonade."

**D
B
T

I N

L I F E**
™

Ways I have made "Lemonade" in the past:

_____

_____

_____

_____

Some of my current lemons are:

_____

_____

_____

_____

Strategies for making my lemons into "Lemonade" are:

_____

_____

_____

_____

Exploring Emotions

By exploring your emotions you can cope, manage, and regulate emotions effectively to avoid problematic behaviors. Remember not to judge emotions. Emotions aren't good or bad, but what you do with them might be.

The Emotion I am exploring is: _____

I feel this emotion in my body by:

_____

The thoughts that typically go along with this emotion are:

_____

Behaviors that I engage in to express this emotion are:

_____

Am I coping & managing this emotion as effectively as possible? _____

If not, I can be more effective by:

_____
_____
_____
_____

D B T   I N   L I F E ™

Emotional Regulation Skills

Ride the Wave

This skill is about learning that our emotions and impulses are always with us, just like the tides. They come and go. They are strong at times and weak at other times. The tides create waves, just like your emotions. Use this skill to harness the energy of your emotions to "Ride the Wave." By being mindfully aware of your emotions, but not acting on them, you can take the energy of the emotion and redirect it in a more effective manner.

D
B
T

I
N

L
I
F
E
™

Ways that I get knocked down and washed over by my emotions:

_____

_____

_____

Ways I can keep my balance to "Ride the Wave" of my emotions:

_____

_____

_____

Riding the wave of my emotions will be useful to me because:

_____

_____

_____

Building Positive Emotions

Here is another opportunity for balance. Use this skill to increase your positive emotions through thoughts, relationships, and activities.

D
B
T

I N

L
I
F
E
™

Activities that bring positive emotions into my awareness:

_____

_____

_____

Thoughts that bring positive emotions into my awareness:

_____

_____

_____

Relationships that bring positive emotions into my awareness:

_____

_____

_____

When I am having a lot of negative emotions, I can balance them out by bringing positive emotions into my awareness by:

_____

_____

_____

Building Positive Emotions

Let's explore how you can use this skill to increase your positive emotions through thoughts, relationships, and activities.

D
B
T

I
N

L
I
F
E
™

Barriers and obstacles to me having positive emotions:

_____

_____

_____

Strategies to overcome these barriers and obstacles:

_____

_____

_____

Ways I can have positive emotions in my life on a regular basis are:

_____

_____

_____

_____

_____

_____

_____

_____

EMOTIONS

This acronym is about coping with and managing emotions effectively.

D
B
T

I
N

L
I
F
E
™

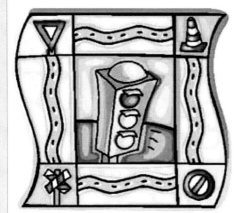

E = Exposure to emotions
M = Mindful of current emotions
O = Outline a plan to deal with emotions
T = Take opposite action
I = Increase positive experiences
O = Obstacles and plan to overcome them
N = Notice what is going on
S = Support system

Exposure to emotions: Spend time with my emotions.

Mindful of current emotions: Build an awareness of what emotions I am feeling in the moment without having to act them out.

Outline a plan to deal with emotions: Figure out how to effectively deal with all of my different emotions.

Take opposite action: Be mindful of my emotion while engaging in the actions that bring the opposite emotion into my experience.

Increase positive experiences: Do things that are enjoyable and fun.

Obstacles and plan to overcome them: Determine the obstacles to effectively deal with my emotions and how to overcome them.

Notice what is going on: Be aware of what was going on around me and inside me.

Support system: Connect with my support system to help me cope.

Emotional Regulation Skills

EMOTIONS

D
B
T

I
N

L
I
F
E
™

I can be **E**xposed to emotions by:

_____

_____

_____

I can be **M**indful of current emotions by:

_____

_____

_____

My **O**utline to deal with emotions is:

_____

_____

_____

I can **T**ake opposite action by:

_____

_____

_____

EMOTIONS

I can **I**ncrease positive experiences by:

_____

_____

_____

I can overcome **O**bstacles by:

_____

_____

_____

I can **N**otice what is going on by:

_____

_____

_____

I can use my **S**upport system by:

_____

_____

_____

_____

D
B
T

I
N

L
I
F
E
™

Emotional Regulation Skills

Opposite to Emotion

This skill is designed to help you reduce the intensity of problematic emotions by engaging in behaviors that bring about the opposite emotion.

D
B
T

I
N

L
I
F
E
™

1. The emotion that I am choosing to make less problematic is:

_____

2. The opposite to this problematic emotions is:

_____

3. Thoughts, actions, and behaviors that bring the opposite emotion into my awareness:

_____

_____

_____

_____

4. Ways I can engage in these thoughts, actions, and behaviors on any given day, in any given situation:

_____

_____

_____

_____

CARES

Using "CARES" to manage my emotions by:

C = Being <u>C</u>alm
A = Monitoring <u>A</u>rousal
R = Finding rest and <u>R</u>elaxation
E = Effectively coping with my <u>E</u>motions
S = Getting a healthy amount of <u>S</u>leep

CARES

I can be <u>C</u>alm by:

_____

_____

_____

I can monitor <u>A</u>rousal by:

_____

_____

_____

I can find rest and <u>R</u>elaxation by:

_____

_____

_____

I can effectively cope with my <u>E</u>motions by:

_____

_____

_____

I can get a healthy amount of <u>S</u>leep by:

_____

_____

_____

D
B
T

I
N

L
I
F
E
™

TRUST

T = <u>T</u>rust myself
R = <u>R</u>edirect my impulses and urges
U = <u>U</u>se my skills
S = Act how I want others to <u>S</u>ee me
T = <u>T</u>ame my emotions and impulses

Emotional Regulation Skills

TRUST

I can Trust myself by:

_____

_____

_____

I can Redirect my impulses and urges by:

_____

_____

_____

I can Use my skills by:

_____

_____

_____

I can act how I want others to See me by:

_____

_____

_____

I can Tame my emotions and impulses by:

_____

_____

_____

MEDDSS

<u>U</u>se
<u>M</u>astery
<u>E</u>xercise
<u>D</u>iet
<u>D</u>rugs (Medication)
<u>S</u>leep
<u>S</u>pirituality
to be skillful.

<u>Mastery</u>: Engage in something or remind yourself of things you are good at. Tap into what you have mastery over.

<u>Exercise</u>: Use exercise to defuse energy and stay healthy. You can stretch, walk, or exercise in ways that are appropriate for your physical condition.

<u>Diet</u>: Eat a balanced diet. Pay particular attention to what your emotions are like when you have a lot of sugar, caffeine, or nicotine.

<u>Drugs (Medication)</u>: Take your prescription drugs as directed and don't use alcohol and illicit drugs.

<u>Sleep</u>: Get a healthy amount of sleep most of the time. Not too much or too little sleep.

<u>Spirituality</u>: Develop a sense of spirituality, connection, and meaning in your life.

Emotional Regulation Skills

MEDDSS

D
B
T

I N

L I F E
™

Use
Mastery
Exercise
Diet
Drugs (Medication)
Sleep
Spirituality
to be skillful

The hardest part of MEDDSS for me is:

_____

_____

Ways I can make it less difficult:

_____

_____

Strategies for practicing MEDDSS in my life on a daily basis are:

_____

_____

_____

_____

BEHAVIOR

B = Use effective **B**ehavior
E = Be grounded in the **E**nvironment
H = Do things that are **H**ealing not hurting
A = **A**ct in my best interests
V = Be consistent with my **V**alues
I = **I**magine getting through difficulties
O = Focus on the desired **O**utcome
R = **R**einforce my successes

D
B
T

I
N

L
I
F
E
™

Emotional Regulation Skills

BEHAVIOR

I can use effective **B**ehavior by:

_____

_____

I can be grounded in the **E**nvironment by:

_____

_____

I can do things that are **H**ealing not hurting by:

_____

_____

I can **A**ct in my best interests by:

_____

_____

BEHAVIOR

I can be consistent with my **V**alues by:

_____

_____

I can **I**magine getting through difficulties by:

_____

_____

I can focus on the desired **O**utcome by:

_____

_____

I can **R**einforce my successes by:

_____

Practicing Emotional Regulation

My favorite emotional regulation skills are:

_____

_____

_____

_____

_____

_____

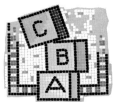

Ways that I use these skills are:

_____

_____

_____

_____

_____

_____

Emotional Regulation Skills

Emotional Regulation Skills Word Search

```
G L B U I L D P O S I T I V E E M O T I O N S
W R K J Q K L P Q V J G J Z R W T Y N R D Q M
G E T T I N G T O K N O W M Y E M O T I O N S
X F F L W B R F K K N F J D G J Q V T J W H D
G N R K O L K Q R B Z Z R B F H T L D J G E N
Z K D N B V R L X R M P H E N T C R L L M X L
K B N K D X E Z H S H M H H T N N A D M F P N
D Z W W P L T D S N Z R E A F R Z V R M M L Y
F N J D T K R D A T T V L V M Q U N Y E R O L
B N P Y L C D R G N A W S I K Q M S K Z S R K
L D T L B E L F R W D N D O D M M K T G V I N
E P R A M K F L E K O E N R N F Y V H R D N L
M V X V C G R H F I N T L Y Q N L V D Z D G M
O R L H G T T Q T K N K D I T K T K Q D B M Q
N T F D F E Z O X H W P H B O V L Y R T P Y N
A X J T D X M G J K L K K T P N M G J K T E J
D R R I T E R C L M X K L K X B S N X H L M D
E P R F E E L I N G N O T A C T I N G N Y O B
M T B T P Z N Z P M P K M T H R R G V V Y T X
L T M K P V R L L P F Y T J Z Z L K G F Q I M
C W P B C R J L H L D X K Q K Q R W Z K K O Q
T V Q V Y R H J D C C C P K R C P C B G R N X
P B H L O P P O S I T E T O E M O T I O N S H
```

DBT IN LIFE™

www.WordSearchMaker.com

ABC | Getting to Know My Emotions
BEHAVIOR | Lemonade
Build Positive Emotions | Love Dandelions
CARES | MEDDSS
EMOTIONS | Opposite to Emotions
Exploring My Emotions | Ride the Wave
Feeling not Acting | TRUST

Emotional Regulation Skills Word Search Answers

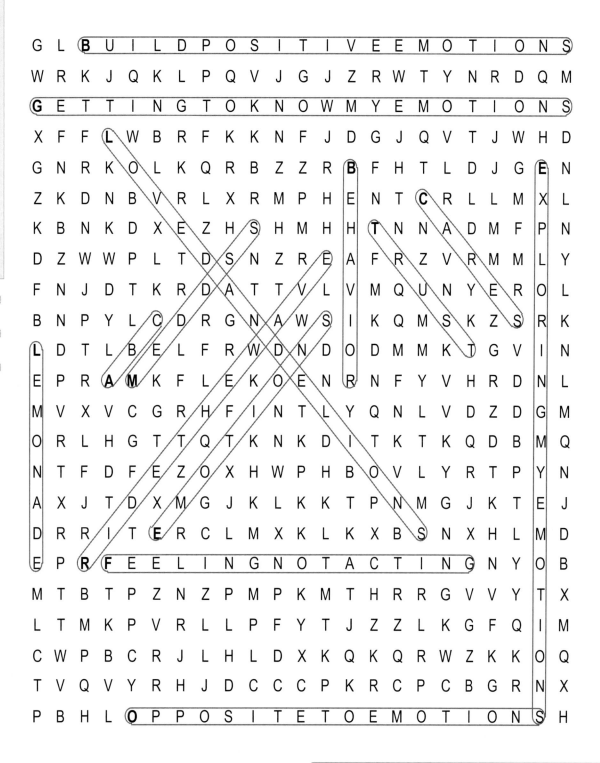

Emotional Regulation Skills Crossword Puzzle

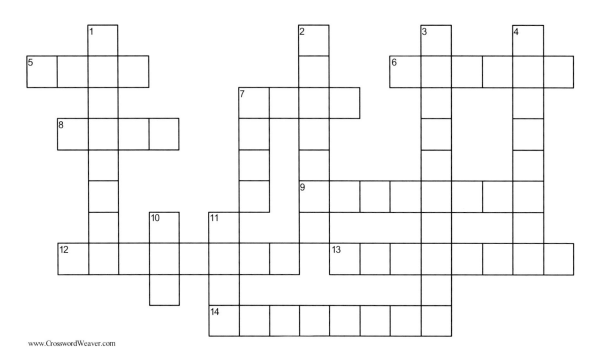

www.CrosswordWeaver.com

D
B
T

I
N

L
I
F
E
™

ACROSS

5 Learning about my emotions is facilitated by using the Getting to _____ My Emotions skill.

6 The V in BEHAVIOR is about acting consistently with my _____.

7 The C in ABC stands for ____ Ahead.

8 The first D in MEDDSS stands for balanced _____.

9 By using skills I can increase my ability to _____ my emotions.

12 _____ is about refocusing my weaknesses into my strength.

13 _____ to Emotion is about engaging in activities that bring the opposing emotion into my experience.

14 I can Explore My _____ to learn about how I experience my feelings.

DOWN

1 Build _____ Emotions is about having enjoyable emotional experiences.

2 The S in EMOTIONS is about _____ System.

3 Love _____ is about accepting the parts of myself that I don't like, but can't get completely rid of.

4 The R in TRUST stands for _____.

7 The C is CARES is about being _____.

10 I can learn impulse control by using the Feeling ___ Acting skill.

11 I can Ride the ____ to let an emotion or strong impulse run its course.

Emotional Regulation Skills Crossword Puzzle Answers

D
B
T

IN

LIFE
™

	P							S			D			R	
K	N	O	W					U		V	A	L	U	E	S
	S				C	O	P	E			N			D	
D	I	E	T		A		P				D			I	
	T				L		O				E			R	
	I				M		R	E	G	U	L	A	T	E	
	V	N	W			T			I			C			
L	E	M	O	N	A	D	E		O	P	P	O	S	I	T	E
		T	V							N					
			E	M	O	T	I	O	N	S					

Emotional Regulation Skills

CHAPTER 7

Interpersonal Effectiveness Worksheets

Interpersonal Effectiveness Skills

Everyone lives their own life in relationships. Relationships may be with family members, friends, roommates, colleagues, classmates, neighbors, teachers, bosses, authority figures, and others. Perhaps one of the most important relationships is with yourself.

Some of these relationships are active and current. Others are in the past. Some are even in your thoughts and memories.

DBT emphasizes that to be effective with all of these relationships, you must be able to get your needs met, invest in relationships, and have self-respect.

Getting what you want is about being assertive, collaborative, and willing to tolerate not getting it your way all of the time.

Being effective in relationships is about investing in others. Self-respect is accomplished by knowing yourself, believing in your self-worth, and having healthy boundaries.

Accomplishing these 3 components of interpersonal effectiveness takes energy, intention, and flexibility. You have to invest in each of these 3 to achieve them all in balance. It is like keeping 3 plates spinning, you have to pay attention to all 3 of them, alternating pushing the plates so that they all continue spinning. If you forget about one or get distracted, then that plate slows down, it falls off and breaks.

Practice these 3 types of interpersonal effectiveness every day.

D.B.T. in Life™

Interpersonal Effectiveness Skills

Being Effective in Relationships

Less effective strategies that get in my way of having what I want in relationships are:

_____

More effective strategies I can use to get what I want in relationships are:

_____

Less effective strategies that get in my way of healthy relationships are:

_____

Effective strategies I can use to have healthy relationships are:

_____

Less effective strategies that get in the way of me having healthy self-respect are:

_____

More effective strategies I can use to have healthy self-respect are:

_____

D.B.T. in Life™

Interpersonal Effectiveness Skills
Broken Record

This skill is about being a "Broken Record" with your self.

Keep coming back to myself.
Keep coming back to my needs.
Keep coming back to my values.
Keep coming back to my self-care.
Keep coming back to who I want to be.
Keep coming back to what I want my life to be like.
Keep coming back to my commitment to having healthy relationships.

The most important things for me to keep coming back to are:

_____

_____

Barriers and obstacles I may encounter to being a "Broken Record":

_____

_____

Strategies I can use to overcome these barriers and obstacles:

_____

_____

Ways I can be a "Broken Record" in my life:

_____

_____

D.B.T. in Life™

Interpersonal Effectiveness Skills

Ignore

While you can practice being non-judgmental with yourself and others on a daily basis, you can't stop others from judging you. However, you can "Ignore" their judgments. You don't have to let these judgments have any impact on you. Also, you can be non-judgmental with those who are judgmental of you, even when it is hard and challenging.

Ways I can "Ignore" the judgments of others:

_____

_____

_____

_____

_____

Ways I can be non-judgmental with others when they are judging me:

_____

_____

_____

_____

_____

D.B.T. in Life™

Interpersonal Effectiveness Skills
Turn the Tables

This skill is about being reciprocal. Since you use your skills to get people to help you, you also have to do things to help others. Sometimes you can contribute without being asked. You can help out even when you don't feel like it, are having bad day, or are experiencing pain.

This skill is about helping out and doing things for others. You may find contributing to be useful and rewarding all on its own. You can do things for others or help out even when you're not getting anything in return. It is helpful to do things for people who have or will help you.

Things that make it hard to "Turn the Tables" in my relationships:

_____

_____

Ways I can minimize what is hard about "Turn the Tables":

_____

_____

Ways I can effectively "Turn the Tables" in my relationships regularly:

_____

_____

Things I can do any day to "Turn the Tables":

_____

_____

D.B.T. in Life™

Interpersonal Effectiveness Skills

Interactions in Relationships

Use this skill to develop frustration tolerance in your interpersonal interactions.

I can observe and describe what is going on in interactions by:

_____

_____

I can be mindful of my emotions by:

_____

_____

I can take a non-judgmental stance in interactions by:

_____

_____

I can use assertive communication by:

_____

_____

I can respect myself and others by:

_____

_____

D.B.T. in Life™

Interpersonal Effectiveness Skills
Relationship Thinking

This skill is designed to help you hold multiple perspectives and viewpoints, because while reality can be black and white, it is mostly shades of grey. In relationships, there is usually a kernel of truth in each person's perspective even when the viewpoints are in conflict.

This skill is about holding a "both/and" perspective in relationships instead of an "either/or" perspective.

This skill is about appreciating other people's opinions, tolerating not always having the answers, and acknowledging making mistakes sometimes.

It is about caring about others even when they annoy you. It is about realizing others care about you, but can be very frustrated with you.

It is about needs and wants; self and others; as well as talking and listening.

Instead of seeing things as "always and never," it is more likely to be way too much and not often enough.

Instead of seeing relationships as "with you or against you," perhaps it can be that others care about you and sometimes do things you disagree with.

This skill is about holding things in balance, tolerating frustrations, and being collaborative in relationships.

D.B.T. in Life™

Interpersonal Effectiveness Skills

Relationship Thinking

You can use this skill to reduce or eliminate black-and-white thinking. This skill fosters dialectical thinking by seeing things from multiple viewpoints and holding a "both/ and" perspective.

Ways I can balance listening and talking:

_____

_____

Ways I can appreciate others' viewpoints:

_____

_____

Ways I can "agree to disagree" with others:

_____

_____

Ways I can stay in relationships even when there are conflicts:

_____

_____

Ways I can think about relationships from a "both/and" perspective:

_____

_____

D.B.T. in Life™

Interpersonal Effectiveness Skills

Relationship Assumptions

1. You are doing the best you can and you can work on being more effective in your relationships.
2. No one has caused all of their problems in relationships and yet you need to solve them anyway.

You can use both of these assumptions to be compassionate, collaborative, and effective in your relationships.

Ways I can apply these assumptions in my relationships are:

_____

_____

_____

_____

D.B.T. in Life™

Interpersonal Effectiveness Skills

Relationship Mindfulness

Use this skill to increase your mindfulness in relationships by being in the moment, non-judgmental, and by focusing on what is most effective.

I can identify generalizations in my relationships by:

_____

_____

I can describe assumptions that I make in my relationships by:

_____

_____

I can suspend judgments I make in my relationships by:

_____

_____

I can avoid jumping to conclusions in my relationships by:

_____

_____

I can be empowered to be effective in my relationships by:

_____

_____

D.B.T. in Life™

Interpersonal Effectiveness Skills

Dealing with Difficult People

Everyone has times when they need to deal with people who are unpleasant or argumentative. This skill is about having the tools to be able to deal with people that are difficult. You can use this skill when dealing with people that you find difficult, challenging, or problematic.

I can be non-judgmental with this relationship by:

_____

_____

I can participate in improving this relationship by:

_____

_____

I can identify and overcome obstacles
to improvement by:

_____

_____

_____

I can stay focused on what is important
in this relationship by:

_____

_____

_____

D.B.T. in Life™

Interpersonal Effectiveness Skills

The Most Difficult

This skill is about dealing with the "Most Difficult" people and relationships. Even when things are challenging and people are hard to deal with, it may be in your best interest to figure out to how to deal with them effectively.

Rate the level of difficulty (0-10) _____

Feelings about this person are:

_____

_____

_____

I can minimize my judgments by:

_____

_____

I can keep my short-term and long-term goals in mind by:

_____

_____

I can engage in effective interactions with difficult people by:

_____

_____

_____

D.B.T. in Life™

Interpersonal Effectiveness Skills

Repairs

This skill is about having healthy relationships that last. Part of this skill is being able to make and accept apologies as well as having the ability to let go sometimes.

While not an easy process, being able to admit when you've made mistakes and were wrong can be very useful. Effectively apologizing will increase trust and safety.

Being able to effectively accept apologies is useful in relationships because it is respectful and compassionate.

Occasionally, letting things go enhances relationships by allowing you to be in the present without bringing in baggage from the past.

D.B.T. in Life™

Interpersonal Effectiveness Skills

Repairs

Ways that apologizing is hard from me:

_____

_____

Strategies that I can use to improve my ability to apologize:

_____

_____

Ways that it is difficult for me to accept apologies from others:

_____

_____

Strategies that I can use to improve my ability to accept apologies:

_____

_____

Ways that it is hard for me to let go:

_____

_____

Strategies that I can use to improve my ability to let go:

_____

_____

D.B.T. in Life™

Interpersonal Effectiveness Skills

4 Horsemen of the Apocalypse

This skill involves identifying the 4 destructive forces each person brings into relationships. Horsemen are things that cause stress and damage relationships. Below are examples of horsemen that both youth and adults may bring to their relationships:

Youth	Adults
• Not communicating • Withdrawal • Dishonesty • Not going to school • Playing video games • Bullying • Violence • Drugs and alcohol • Delinquency	• Dishonesty • Not taking mental health meds • Out-of-control spending • Credit card debt • Workaholism • Drugs and alcohol • Compulsive or Addictive Behaviors • Violence • Infidelity

One important rule with the "4 Horsemen" is that each person is responsible for their own horsemen. Pointing out others' horsemen is provocative and potentially argumentative. It is more effective for each person to focus on his or her own horsemen.

D.B.T. in Life™

Interpersonal Effectiveness Skills

My Horsemen

The most destructive forces that I am at risk of bringing into my relationships are:

_____

_____

Ways I can identify when these forces have snuck in:

_____

_____

Strategies that I can use to keep these forces out of my relationships:

_____

_____

Strategies to reduce or eliminate these horsemen in my life to benefit me and my relationships:

_____

_____

_____

_____

_____

D.B.T. in Life™

Interpersonal Effectiveness Worksheets

Interpersonal Effectiveness Skills

GIVE

This skill is designed to increase your capacities to improve and sustain relationships in healthy ways.

G = **G**entle in relationships
I = **I**nterest in others
V = **V**alidate
E = **E**asy Manner

D.B.T. in Life™

Interpersonal Effectiveness Skills

GIVE

I can be **G**entle in my relationships by:
_____
_____
_____
_____

I can be **I**nterested in others by:
_____
_____
_____

I can **V**alidate others by:
_____
_____
_____

I can have an **E**asy Manner by:
_____
_____
_____

D.B.T. in Life™

Interpersonal Effectiveness Skills

FAST

Self-respect is the goal of this skill. This skill helps you balance investing in others and yourself.

F = <u>F</u>air to self
A = <u>A</u>pologize less
S = <u>S</u>tick to values
T = <u>T</u>ruthful with self

D.B.T. in Life™

Interpersonal Effectiveness Skills

FAST

I can be <u>F</u>air to myself in my relationships by:

_____

_____

_____

I can <u>A</u>pologize less in my relationships by:

_____

_____

_____

I can <u>S</u>tick to values in my relationships by:

_____

_____

_____

I can be <u>T</u>ruthful with myself and others by:

_____

_____

_____

_____

_____

_____

D.B.T. in Life™

Interpersonal Effectiveness Skills

DEAR WOMAN

This skill is designed to help you ask for help or accomplish a task.

D = **D**escribe what is wanted
E = **E**ncourage others to help
A = **A**sk for what is wanted
R = **R**einforce others

W = **W**illingness to tolerate not always getting it my way
O = **O**bserve what is going on inside and around me
M = **M**indfully present in the current moment
A = **A**ppear Confident
N = **N**egotiate with others

D.B.T. in Life™

Interpersonal Effectiveness Skills
DEAR WOMAN

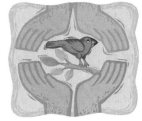

I can **D**escribe what I want by:

_____

I can **E**ncourage others to help me by:

_____

I can **A**sk for what I want by:

_____

I can **R**einforce others by:

_____

I can have **W**illingness to tolerate not always getting it my way by:

_____

I can **O**bserve what is going on inside and around me by:

_____

I can be **M**indfully present in the current moment by:

_____

I can **A**ppear Confident by:

_____

I can **N**egotiate with others by:

_____

D.B.T. in Life™

Interpersonal Effectiveness Skills

DEAR MAN

This skill is designed to help you accomplish a task or ask for help.

D = **D**escribe what is wanted
E = **E**ncourage others to help
A = **A**sk for what is wanted
R = **R**einforce others

M = **M**indfully present in the current moment
A = **A**ppear Confident
N = **N**egotiate with others

D.B.T. in Life™

Interpersonal Effectiveness Skills
DEAR MAN

I can **D**escribe what I want by:

_____

_____

I can **E**ncourage others to help me by:

_____

_____

I can **A**sk for what I want by:

_____

_____

I can **R**einforce others by:

_____

_____

I can be **M**indfully present in the current moment by:

_____

_____

I can **A**ppear Confident by:

_____

_____

I can **N**egotiate with others by:

_____

_____

Interpersonal Effectiveness Skills

This worksheet is designed to help you explore reasons for changing or staying the same in relationships

Pros of keeping my relationships the same	Cons of changing my relationships
Cons of keeping my relationships the same	**Pros of** changing my relationships

Interpersonal Effectiveness Skills

My favorite Interpersonal Effectiveness skills are:

_____

_____

_____

_____

Ways that I use these skills are:

_____

_____

_____

_____

Interpersonal Effectiveness Skills Word Search

```
G R L I F Z L L N D Q P J G K D M K Q Z K Y Y T D H F
F E F N V T Y K Z H Q T P K R Q L M V P C C L P E W T
W L T T M K V L M K M T R O K R W N V W T L N T A R B
R A K E R M Q M M R J P C Z L J D Z C L G Y L R L E K
P T M R N Q M M G Z P E M N N D L B U V M D G Q I L X
T I R A M T D C D B R C N T K N E C D R R L B Q N A G
G O E C T Q M L G N N V Q Q H X I A D C H D N J G T X
J N L T T B J V E M P T R C H F F F R K L M C R W I L
Z S A I F M Q K W T W W P R F Q J N D W F L E T I O X
J H T O T O O K T R V K G I H J T R B T O V R G T N Y
K I I N M R U B B R D Z D X H T R F P K I M Z Y H S T
Z P O S B L R R N C Z T H T V N T L N G D T A M D H H
P A N I M V C K H L S P L V K X J R H C X F T N I I L
B S S N R M M M M O T V R C W N C T K K T R N N F P P
L S H R N G H G M M R T L K P R L Q W Y D F F Z F M H
F U I E K C T E T N G S U H F H L B P W Y Y C J I I R
N M P L D D H R V C D T E R T F Q Y J K V N K H C N K
R P T A T T J V H M K J Q M N L D T H Y Y B Y P U D N
G T H T V H L M I G N O R E E T N Z J W J D T W L F M
T I I I Z G C D M D N M T T X N H K Z Z M R V B T U R
M O N O L N C F P R C T G V F L R E T V F B N J P L C
T N K N N D L X F A S T C X K Q X T V W R K N E N B
Z S I S J Z T C V L R T L R D W L N P A M P R N O E F
R M N H M L R P X W M R W L B T J L L V B L R K P S K
R Q G I X K L Z W C C K Y R J Y N R P R W L F R L S H
G R E P A I R S Z Q D T Y M F Q H J K J L K E Y E Q G
C N K S R K L Z F P P W K B Z D K N T N Q N C S P K F
```

www.WordSearchMaker.com

Broken Record	Interactions in Relationships
Dealing with Difficult People	Relationship Assumptions
DEAR WOMAN	Relationship Mindfulness
FAST	Relationship Thinking
Four Horsemen	Repairs
GIVE	The Most Difficult
Ignore	Turn the Tables

D.B.T. in Life™

Interpersonal Effectiveness Skills Word Search Answers

```
G R L I F Z L L N D Q P J G K D M K Q Z K Y Y T D H F
F E F N V T Y K Z H Q T P K R Q L M V P C C L P E W T
W L T T M K V L M K M T R O K R W N V W T L N T A R B
R A K E R M Q M M R J P C Z L J D Z C L G Y L R L E K
P T M R N Q M M G Z P E M N N D L B U V M D G Q I L X
T I R A M T D C D B R C N T K N E C D R R L B Q N A G
G O E C T Q M L G N N V Q Q H X I A D C H D N J G T X
J N L T T B J V E M P T R C H F F F R K L M C R W I L
Z S A I F M Q K W T W W P R F Q J N D W F L E T I O X
J H T O T O K T R V K G I H J T R B T O V R G T N S T
K I I N M R U B B R D Z D X H T R F P K I M Z Y H S T
Z P O S B L R R N C Z T H T V N T L N G D T A M D H H
P A N I M V C K H L S P L V K X J R H C X F T N I I L
B S S N R M M M O T V R C W N C T K K T R N N F P P P
L S H R N G H G M M R T L K P R L Q W Y D F F Z F M H
F U I E K C T E T N G S U H F H L B P W Y Y C J I I R
N M P L D D H R V C D T E R T F Q Y J K V N K H C N K
R P T A T T J V H M K J Q M N L D T H Y Y B Y P U D N
G T H T V H L M I G N O R E E T N Z J W J D T W L F M
T I I I Z G C D M D N M T T X N H K Z Z M R V B T U C
M O N O L N C F P R C T G V F L R E T V F B N J P L C
T N K N N N D L X F A S T C X K Q X T V W R K N E N B
Z S I S J Z T C V L R T L R D W L N P A M P R N O E F
R M N H M L R P X W M R W L B T J L L V B L R K P S K
R Q G I X K L Z W C C K Y R J Y N R P R W L F R L S H
G R E P A I R S Z Q D T Y M F Q H J K J L K E Y E Q G
C N K S R K L Z F P P W K B Z D K N T N Q N C S P K F
```

D.B.T. in Life™

Interpersonal Effectiveness Skills Crossword Puzzle

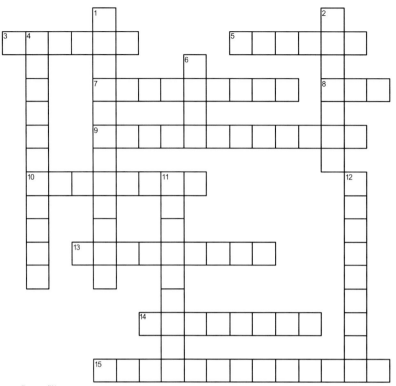

www.CrosswordWeaver.com

ACROSS

3 The Turn the _____ skill about is about helping out and being reciprocal.

5 I can be a _____ Record with myself by keep coming back to my needs.

7 The A in FAST is for _____ less.

8 When I use the Repairs skill, I can apologize, accept apologies and ___ go of some things.

9 _____ in Relationships is about avoiding generalizations when dealing with others.

10 Relationship _____ helps me appreciate other people's perspectives.

13 The Most _____ gives me tools to interact with the people I find the hardest to deal with.

14 The V in GIVE stands for _____.

15 The skills in this category help me have Interpersonal _____ by helping me get what I want in relationships, sustaining relationships, and maintaining my self-respect.

DOWN

1 _____ Mindfulness is about being in the here and now with my support system.

2 _____ with Difficult People helps me be in relationship with people that are problematic for me.

4 Relationship _____ is about acknowledging that we are are all doing the best we can and that we can be more effective by using our DBT skills.

6 I can figure out the most destructive forces I bring into my relationships by using the _____ Horsemen skill.

11 The N in DEAR WOMAN stands for _____.

12 When I use the Ignore skill I can ignore other people's _____ of me.

D.B.T. in Life™

Interpersonal Effectiveness Skills Crossword Puzzle Answers

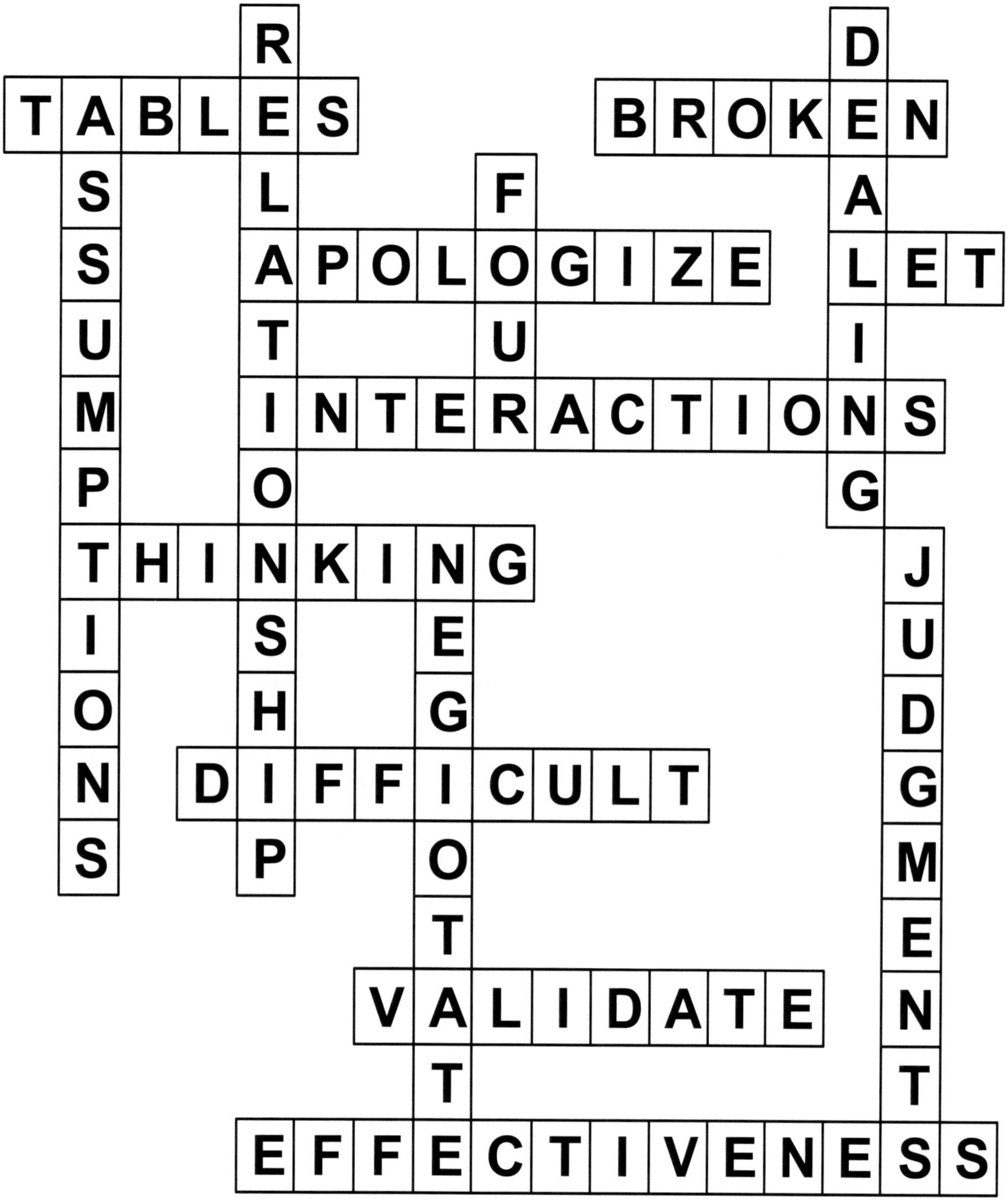

Crossword grid answers:

- TABLES
- RELATIONSHIP
- BROKEN
- DEALING
- ASSUMPTIONS
- APOLOGIZE
- LET
- FUGUE
- INTERACTIONS
- THINKING
- JUDGMENT
- REGIOTT
- DIFFICULT
- VALIDATE
- EFFECTIVENESS

D.B.T. in Life™

Interpersonal Effectiveness Skills

D.B.T. in Life™

References

Linehan, Marsha M. (1993a). *Cognitive-behavioral treatment of borderline personality disorder.* Guilford Press: New York.

Linehan, Marsha M. (1993b). *Skills training manual for treating borderline personality disorder.* Guilford Press: New York.

Mara, Thomas, (2004). *Depressed & Anxious: The dialectical behavior therapy workbook for overcoming depression and anxiety.* New Harbinger Press: Oakland.

Mara, Thomas, (2005). *Dialectical behavior therapy in private practice: A practical and comprehensive guide.* New Harbinger Press: Oakland.

Moonshine, Cathy (2007). *Advanced Dialectical Behavior Therapy.* Eau Claire, WI: PESI. (Available at http://www.pesi.com)

Spradlin, Scott E. (2003). *Don't let your emotions run your life: How dialectical behavior therapy can put you in control.* New Harbinger Press: Oakland.

Notes

Notes

Notes